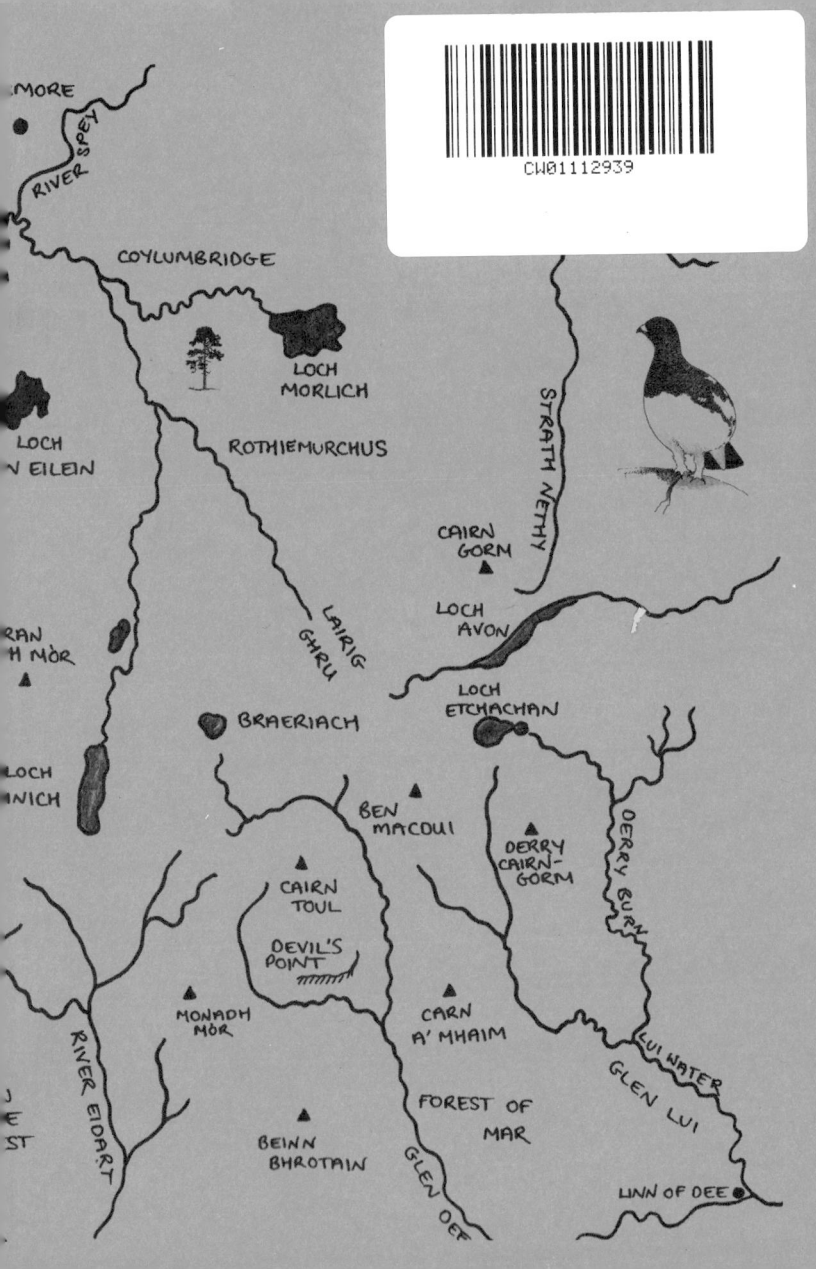

A Cairngorm Chronicle

A F Whyte

A CAIRNGORM CHRONICLE

illustrated by Rose Shawe-Taylor

Millrace

First published in Great Britain in 2007 by
Millrace
2a Leafield Road, Disley
Cheshire SK12 2JF
www.millracebooks.co.uk

A F Whyte's text © 2007 Anne Thoms
Illustrations © 2007 Rose Shawe-Taylor
Endpaper maps © 2007 Jane Droop

All rights reserved. No part of this publication may be reproduced, stored in a retrieval system, or transmitted in any form or by any means, electronic, mechanical, photocopying or otherwise, without the prior permission of the copyright holder.

The Author's estate has asserted Alexander Frederick Whyte's moral right under the Copyright, Designs and Patents Act 1988, to be identified as the Author of this Work.

Rose Shawe-Taylor has asserted her moral right under the Copyright, Designs and Patents Act 1988, to be identified as the Illustrator of this Work.

ISBN: 978-1-902173-238

Typeset in Adobe Garamond Pro.
Printed and bound in the United Kingdom
by MPG Books Ltd, Victoria Square, Bodmin, Cornwall.

Alexander Frederick Whyte

Contents

Acknowledgements — ix

Foreword by the Author's Daughter — xi

Introduction — xiii

Preamble: The Challenge of Fuji — 1

One: The Greater Richness — 11

Two: Cairn Gorm — 25

Three: Four Peaks Circuit — 37

Four: The Lairig Ghru — 109

Epilogue: The Curtain Falls in Glen Einich — 143

Appendix I: The Herring Bap & Old Moorland — 149

Appendix II: Putting Allt Eggie on the Map — 153

Author's Acknowledgements

The writer who sets out to acknowledge his debt to others has usually an easy task. Mine is not easy, partly because the debt is great and owed to many, partly because my memory (once reliable) is now not good. But, whether I can now recall (or not) all those to whom I owe some debt, I can at least acknowledge the debts I know.

The greatest is to these hills themselves, but since it would never have been contracted but for one man, I place his name first: William Peyton, Free Church minister, geologist and humanist, who led me amongst them years ago as a child. No other debt challenges his but, as I owe something to others, I record the remaining small charge of obligation to my daughter Joan, as companion on many outings, and her husband John Mackay as the taker of some good pictures; to R B Thomson of Newtonmore for guidance to Meall na Cuaigh and to other summits; to sundry members of the Cairngorm Club and especially to James A Parker, formerly Chief Engineer of the GNER but chiefly a climber, whom I never met but who, a year or two before his death, read the manuscript of this book with critical interest and sent me five pages of comment, with most of which I disagree; to the Reverend A E Robertson of the Scottish Mountaineering Club, who might have taken William Peyton's place in my memory if I had met him earlier; to a disabled ptarmigan who led me into one corner of the Cairngorms which (without his guidance) I would never have seen; to a herd of deer on the shoulder of Sron na Banrigh, and particularly to the leading stag who gave me a sight never forgotten; to Robert Adam; to William Poucher; to the Geological Survey and the Ordnance Survey.

A F Whyte

Publisher's Acknowledgements

Millrace would like to thank Anne Thoms for suggesting this project, for giving access to her father's photographs and for providing a foreword and the biographical information used in the introduction. Thanks, too, to the Cairngorm Club for kind permission to include the extract on pages 19-20, taken from P A Spalding's article in *The Cairngorm Club Journal*, December 1940.

Foreword
by the Author's Daughter

This chronicle was written over sixty years ago, begun in London in December 1943 and added to in 1944, 1945 and 1947. I first saw it in 1971, when I had the melancholy task, with my brother Tony, of emptying the London flat where our parents, Fred and Emy Whyte, had lived for thirty years. I had never heard of the manuscript and believe that Fred had made no attempt to publish it. It is clear from his quotation of John Bunyan's 'Apology' that he wrote for his own pleasure. I decided to leave the work untouched until, in 2004, my granddaughter Lisa Oyama chose The Cairngorm National Nature Reserve as a special subject in her 'Higher Still' exams.

The original runs in one continuous narrative, with many paragraph headings, and includes an account of a twenty-four hour circuit of the High Plateau and Four Peaks in June 1904. The edited text is now presented in four chapters, with a preamble and epilogue; two walks in the 1930s have been cut. A few old photographs were filed with the manuscript, some of which have been used as a basis for Rose Shawe-Taylor's illustrations.

Anne Thoms
Edinburgh, January 2007

The Author's Apology for his Book
The Pilgrim's Progress
by John Bunyan

When at first I took my pen in hand
Thus for to write, I did not understand
That I at all should make a little book
In such a mode…
…But yet I did not think
To show to all the world my pen and ink
In such a mode. I only thought to make
I know not what. Nor did I undertake
Thereby to please my neighbours. No, not I.
I did it mine own self to gratify.
Neither did I but vacant seasons spend
In this my scribble. Nor did intend
But to divert myself in doing this
From worser thoughts which make me do amiss.
Thus I set Pen to Paper with delight,
And quickly had my thoughts in black and white.
For having now my Method by the end,
Still as I pull'd, it came and so I penned
It down, until it came at last to be
For length and breadth the bigness which you see.

Introduction

Before dawn on a June day in 1904, three young men set off from the Shelter Stone. By the time they reached the Dell of Rothiemurchus at the end of the day, they had covered thirty-eight miles and climbed 9,300 feet and nine Munros.

That expedition forms the centrepiece of *A Cairngorm Chronicle,* one man's homage to his favourite mountains. The book stretches over fifty years, from the end of the nineteenth century to the close of the Second World War. Other chapters recall other outings and digress into byways of history and language. In a note, the author makes it clear that the pieces were written over many years. Most were prompted by nostalgia for days on the hills or by outright homesickness as he travelled around the world in the course of a distinguished career. The various parts were finally fitted together between 1943 and 1947.

Some were actually written in the midst of the Cairngorms themselves, huddling against the cairn in a hailstorm or sitting in the upper bothy of Glen Einich, coaxing the reluctant peat fire, scribbling on scraps of paper, on the backs of old envelopes, in hurried hieroglyphics on the linen binding of the Ordnance Survey map ... Others were written far from Mar and

Badenoch, in letters from the East, when the need to be at home again was strong and it was natural to fill the page with 'Do you remember that day on Carn Toul?' But most of them were written not to be read by any other eye, in Simla, in the Conte Rosso on the Indian Ocean, on board Yangtze river steamers, and one part of them, the parent of the comparison with other mountain ranges, was provoked by Fuji himself during a passage through the Inland Sea of Japan.

Although travel was to play such a major part in his later life, Alexander Frederick Whyte's childhood and upbringing were firmly Scottish. He was born in Edinburgh in 1883, the son of the renowned minister, Dr Alexander Whyte,* and Jane Barbour, daughter of a Highland landowner. He was educated at Edinburgh Academy and Edinburgh University, where he gained a first class degree in modern languages. In 1910, aged 26, he was elected Liberal MP for Perth, the youngest MP at the time, and became Parliamentary Private Secretary to Winston Churchill (then First Lord of the Admiralty). In 1912 he married Margaret Emily Fairweather. Their three children, Joan, Anne and Tony, were born in 1914, 1917, and 1921.

Whyte's career as an MP ended when constituency changes abolished his seat in 1919. He turned to journalism, attending the Paris Peace Conference for the *Daily*

*For an account of Dr Whyte's remarkable rise from humble beginnings, see Anne Thoms' autobiography, A Journey through the Twentieth Century, *Minerva Press 1996.*

News, lecturing on foreign affairs and founding and editing *The New Europe* magazine. In 1920 he was appointed president of the newly formed Legislative Assembly of India, for which he was knighted. When the five-year appointment came to an end, he turned down offers of the governorships of Madras and Bombay and returned to journalism and lecturing. He travelled widely in the Far East, as political adviser to the National Government of China, and in the United States. From 1939 to 1940 he was head of the American Division of the Ministry of Information. He was involved with the BBC Brains Trust, worked for the Royal Institute of International Affairs and was awarded an honorary LLD from Edinburgh University and degrees from the US universities McGill, Michigan and Dartmouth. His publications include *Asia in the 20th Century* (1926), *China and Foreign Powers* (1927) and *The Future of East and West* (1932).

Throughout this successful, globe-trotting career, Whyte's affection for the Cairngorms, rooted in childhood visits and maturing on later expeditions, remained strong. He never lost the light-hearted enthusiasm and anticipation that he first felt playing a game of Robbers' Cave on Cairn Gorm with William Peyton, and that sense of fun frequently surfaces in *A Cairngorm Chronicle*. He is the mountains' staunch advocate, delighting in their uncommon beauty and history, and applauding their modest refusal to put all their goods in the shop window.

Above all, he is fascinated by the close interweaving of land and language, and the way the Gaelic has evolved in response to a subtle and complex terrain. He stresses repeatedly the importance of place-names and the profound interest to be found in tracing their evolution: 'There is plenty of the explorer's zest ... in pursuing to their origin the *authentic* names of stream and corrie in the Cairngorms.' There is plenty of fun in inauthentic naming, too: on another expedition in 1904, he and his friends ceremonially christen an anonymous stream and embark on a chase to track its source. Later, in the follow-up to this episode (Appendix II, 'Putting Allt Eggie on the Map'), Whyte makes fun of his linguistic hobby-horse and academic and literary pretensions.

Inevitably, the long period over which the book was written has led to unevenness in the text. The preamble in which Whyte defends the Cairngorms against the world's great mountains perhaps relies too heavily—for modern taste, at least—on rhetorical device and literary allusion. But, as the book progresses, he gets into his stride, his learning is worn more lightly and his sense of humour emerges. He is at his most relaxed when out on the hills, trading quips and quotations with his companions in those heady, innocent days of 1904. One of these companions, Hugh Miller, was the grandson of the famous geologist of the same name; the identity of the other (McGilky was not, apparently, his real name) is unknown. As the three range contentedly over the plateau, stopping to light their pipes or soap their socks, arguing about which mountains they can see or giving geological names to Scottish football teams, there is a keen sense of enjoyment, adventure and unsentimental male camaraderie that is reminiscent of a John Buchan novel. Indeed, Buchan, another Scottish churchman's son who made his mark on the international stage, was almost a contemporary.

At his best, Whyte writes compellingly and well. Over a century after the event, his words still conjure up the vigour and *joie de vivre* of that long, sunny day in June 1904 when he, Miller and McGilky made their grand circuit, taking in Cairn Gorm, Ben Macdui, Carn a' Mhaim, Beinn Bhrotain, Monadh Mor, Devil's Point, Cairn Toul, Sgor an Lochain Uaine and Braeriach. At the time it was an almost unheard-of accomplishment, though, looking back in the 1940s, Whyte noted ruefully, 'The four main tops have been climbed so often in one day that the feat is no longer worthy of record.' He underrated himself.

Preamble
The Challenge of Fuji

Let me commence at the moment when I first saw Fujiyama and was, as it were, challenged by him to declare any claim of the Cairngorms which could hold a candle to him. 'Avoid giving of characters,' said the Puritan divine. 'Comparisons are odious,' echoed the old saying. And yet… and yet… The Cairngorms egg us on to become their partisans. They challenge comparison with other mountain ranges—and challenge them without fear.

We are all like the man from Nithsdale who returned from the East and was found gazing down at the stream from the bridge in the town of Dumfries. As men will, he was murmuring to himself. And a passer-by stopped to listen.

'Na, na. T'was an awfu' lee, ay, an awfu' lee!'
'What?' said the passer-by.
'Ah said that the Hooghly at Calcutta wasnae as braid's the Nith at Dumfries. It was an awfu' lee, but Ah'm glad Ah said it.'

We have all, at our chosen moment, been 'glad Ah

said it'. And since Fuji challenged the comparison, and summoned the lofty and massive peaks of Europe and Asia to support him, let him have it.

It is true that these Scottish mountains are low in stature compared with the giants of the earth. When Agricola fought his battle of Mons Graupius he may well have thought it was but a little mound compared with the mass of his own Alps.* The Cairngorms do not possess the piercing and dramatic grandeur of the Alps and they are quite innocent of the rather histrionic pose of their Swiss rivals. Nor have they the continental massiveness of the Sierras and the Rocky Mountains that shut the dull North American plain from the loveliest part of that not always lovely continent. Nor, again, can any pass in the Grampians hope to challenge the Yangtze Gorges for depth and mystery and awe. But the comparison-maker must walk warily here—for it is precisely in these western Chinese mountains that we come nearer than anywhere else to the quality of the Cairngorms. How this trick of affinity is played by Nature, who can say? Yet it *is* played.

According to Tacitus, Agricola, the Roman Governor of Britain AD77–83/4, confronted the Caledonian tribes led by Calgacus on the Graupian Mountain somewhere in north-east Scotland.

But Fuji has other witnesses to bring. He still has the great uplands of Asia to support him against the complacent claim of the Cairngorms. He reminds us that, not only in peak and precipice but in the vast expanse of the high desert, there is a mighty and multitudinous manifestation unequalled anywhere. And, finally, he throws on the screen the unforgettable skyline of the Himalayas, etched against the clearing monsoon sky, when the sharp air of autumn gives the new snow a piercing brightness and there falls on every summit a light that never was on sea or land. On this cumulative evidence, the case is unanswerable and no answer need be attempted.

Are these comparisons? Hardly. For the Latin origin of our word implies equality, things that stand on a par with one another. This the Cairngorms implicitly and explicitly deny. Rivals they may admit, with a kind of arrogant tolerance in the act. Contrasts they welcome and, in welcoming them, bid us again to remember our Latin—for the word means 'standing out against'. But, of course, this is an idle debate.

God gave all men all earth to love,
But since our hearts are small
Ordained for each one spot should prove
Beloved over all…

The poet found his one spot in Sussex. Others have created their earth in other shires, some because they were born there and grew deeper-rooted to the soil from which they sprung, and some because, like the poet, they only found their final moorings after world-wide wanderings. In the same poem there is the line 'Choose ye your need from Thames to Tweed'—thereby leaving all Scotland out of the choice, perhaps because Rudyard Kipling wanted a rhyme or, being very English, forgot the north.

However that may be, the 'need' is domestic. All these choosers, the poet included, chose their one spot as the site of home and fireside. We are on another quest. We are drawn to the Cairngorms and held by them in an altogether different way—drawn to them, but not as to slippered ease under the oak rafters of Bateman's. The Cairngorms are home indeed, but in an almost other-worldly sense: the home of the spirit, the shrine to which the wanderer returns to recapture that which he dare not lose.

Here, then, is no matter for comparison. We may come home again, not ungrateful to Fuji for the challenge that sent us sightseeing among the great mountains of the world. And as we return, we rejoice to know that, despite all Fuji's efforts, Cairngorm withers are unwrung. Just as the traveller returning to Edinburgh sees her old magic with new eyes, so the Cairngorms take new hold on us after we have seen their many rivals under foreign skies.

There are varying ways to approach and differing standards to apply to all mountains. Polonius would tell us that we may choose between the historical–geological, the geological–mineralogical, the mineralogical–meteorological and so forth, but our appreciation of the Cairngorms is neither historical alone, geological alone, nor merely mineralogical—being, as it were, a portrait in a mirror, the mirror held up to Nature by the hand of a child. By the same token, this is the mirror of one individual mind. The reflection of these hills in my mirror will probably not tally exactly with their story as told by the great geologists, nor with their portrait in your mirror. It could hardly be otherwise.

To take but one instance which sounds like scientific observation: these mountains look solid, more solid than any others. (If you doubt it, look at Carn Toul, even in a photograph.) They have a certain stereoscopic quality by which you may look round the corner and see more than the camera would reveal. The common phrase has it that 'they stand out' from themselves and from their background, and this seeing-round-the-corner gives them at once their solidity and their elusive ethereal loveliness. But, if they 'stand out', they also 'stand in'. They are linked and married, the one to the other, so that their 'standing out' means no separation, but a kind of individual identification of each other as members of one another. It is not only that the Cairngorms would indeed be a broken arc if one of them were so removed from his fellows, but that they all partake of the same quality, bearing so strong a family likeness—a likeness wholly their own, unshared by other ranges—that their individual characters are less salient in their portrait than their perfect community. They are a 'scene individable'.

We shall see how individual each can be. We shall find ourselves divided in partisanship for one peak against another with, perhaps, a shameless favouritism. But, before we take them one by one, something more may be said about their special trick of focusing themselves, not as lines against the sky but as objects in stereoscope. And here I find myself going back to Fuji. There is no better instance of the contrast between those who let you see-round-the-corner and those who do not than Fujisan and the Cairngorms. It may be unjust to say that Fuji's volcanic cone is flat, for he has a rounded air. Nonetheless, neither in the monsoon, which can play stereoscopic tricks, nor in the transparent air of the fall, does Fuji appear to have more than two dimensions. He is like a delicate watercolour painted on a blue background, and in many of Hiroshige's prints of the Tokkaido Road he appears like the leitmotif which accompanies the traveller on that Japanese highway. You could not treat the Cairngorms in such fashion. They are 'whole as the marble, founded as the rock'. They are not to be enclosed in the tracery of a Japanese screen, though I could imagine a Japanese artist taking the twin tops of Carn Toul and using the unbroken sweep from the

The Cairngorms: the Lairig Ghru

summit to the Dee much as his fellows have used the graceful curve of Fujiyama. It would be a study in line and colour, drawn with a certain formalism in obedience to convention and keeping spontaneity well controlled in the harness of tradition. Perspective would be limited in its effect and subordinated to the Japanese conception of artistic design. Everything that is vital to the depiction of mass and power in the Cairngorms would be held severely in check. One is tempted to speculate whether it is because Fuji seems to look like that, or whether artistic orthodoxy requires him to be so treated, that one always thinks of him as lacking his third dimension.

The Cairngorms, in their physical shape, in their outstanding and complete roundedness and in the thoughts they suggest, are not only filled out in their three dimensions but have a four-dimensional quality as well. This is more difficult to define, for we are now passing almost beyond the borders of the finite to where figure and form become transfigured. What we see before us in the Cairngorms will partake of all the physical stuff of granite and quartz, mica and well-coloured precious stone, but chiefly the 'poem unlimited'. And if poetry be indeed the image in the eye passed through the lens of the mind's eye and transformed by the prism of the imagination, then, confronted by our own impotence to define the vision in common terms, we must seek expression in poetry. Like all such manifestations, this is at once an outward and an inward experience: a dazzling physical sight and a moving of the mind within. Consciously felt it may not be, perhaps, but few indeed are the frequenters of these hills who at *some* moment have not come under their spell in this manner. It is as if they were, in themselves, poet and poem at once.

Be that as it may. This is but one testimony among a thousand to the nature of the spell cast by the Cairngorms. It is an impress on the mind, like the design on the face of a coin. The image in the eye changes every hour but the image in the mind's eye only grows clearer, more indelibly impressed. You may need to take the one-inch map from the shelf a hundred times to refresh your memory of the exact relation of this corrie and that, or measure again the precise distance you once walked in tracing the Luineag from her source in the No Man's Land between Corrie Dhondail and the Angel's Peak. But this image on the mind's eye is not on any map, for it is the transformation of the story told by the map into something rich and strange.

That transformation is of the essence and nature of poetry, poetry in its deepest and richest Shakespearean sense. The parallels which these mountains suggest and the feelings they evoke belong to the Shakespearean range of thought and emotion, partaking at once of the magnanimous and the intimate. There is a universality in Shakespeare which, at first sight, would seem to preclude the ordinary man's sharing in his thought. Yet we know the ordinary man can and does. No remoteness separates the poet and his reader. And with the Cairngorms, neither their universality nor their apparent remoteness has ever removed them to that impersonal distance which so often separates puny man from the more grandiose wonders of Nature in other parts of the world.

These are Scottish hills, standing in a climate which colours and enriches their own innate gravity and maturity, presenting them in an atmosphere and through a mediating light which surround no other mountains in the world. To diagnose the state of mind created by them or to transfer the image from the mind's eye to the written word is a formidable, well-nigh impossible task. Only the great poet himself could perform it.

One
The Greater Richness

Those who have lived longest under the shadow of the Cairngorms and know them best have found that their variety makes so many different impressions on the mind that a fitting mountain vocabulary is required to describe them. Hence the greater richness in the naming of what they saw by the Gaelic speakers who first gave names to these hills—a wealth far greater than the English language possesses. As P A Spalding says, the Highlanders had 'a highly developed sense of mountain *form*; nor did they lack words to distinguish what they saw.' The climber whose mother tongue is English is often at a disadvantage for, though he may use the Gaelic name for a shoulder or a corrie, he will likely miss its significance. And there is plenty of room for confusion in the place-names of the Cairngorms. Most of them passed into general use by word of mouth, changing the sound and accent as they passed. They became common coin of the mountain folk before ever they were written, far less printed, and therefore when the

Ordnance Survey took up the task of mapping and naming these peaks and streams, they had to deal not only with two languages but with many varieties of name and pronunciation in the Gaelic alone. This stimulating uncertainty may have begun with Tacitus and his unlocated Mons Graupius, but it lasted for eighteen centuries after the Roman historian and still provokes much ingenuity, in which the Ordnance Survey takes no part but steers its own safe course.

More than once, a certain Dr Pont, Master of Arts of the University of St Andrews ('capped' in 1584) is quoted as the authority for some of the earliest known names of these hills. This Timothy Pont was an accomplished mathematician and a topographer who made, or projected, an Atlas of Scotland and, by the testimony of the Curator of the National Library in Edinburgh, drew his own maps for the sixteenth-century forerunner of the Ordnance Survey—quaint and uncertain drawings to be seen to this day at Parliament House. He was the elder son of Robert Pont (variously spelt 'Pont', 'Kylpont', and 'Kynpont') who was made Commissioner for the Kirk in the shires of Moray, Banff and Inverness in 1563 when little Tim was three years old. We can guess that the son would ply his father with questions about 'thae muckle braes ower yonder' and, receiving chilling replies from his ecclesiastical parent, would resolve in his secret mind of childhood to find the answers himself one of those days.

And find them he did, as far as a sixteenth-century inquirer could. But these maps of old Timothy's design show that he never pushed far into the Cairngorms, which doubtless he knew generically as 'the Mounth'. They portray the hills merely as a general mass which no sensible men would penetrate, there being nothing to be found within them. Only two Cairngorm outposts stand marked on Master Pont's map: 'Ben Arvin', which we can recognise as our own Ben Avon (or A'an), and Mons Biniwroden, not quite so recognisable but nonetheless the Pontine name of Ben Bhrottain. All of which goes to show that the topographer of this sixteenth-century Atlas of Scotland never saw the Cairngorms from Badenoch.

And, be it remembered, the mapping of the Cairngorms is a comparatively recent operation. The sixteenth century had few names for these hills; the seventeenth was little better and small wonder, for men of taste gave this inaccessible 'Mounth' a wide berth. And there were English travellers in Shakespeare's time who could say that *the men of old did no more wonder that the great Messias should be borne in so poor a towne as Bethlehem in Judia, than I do wonder that as King James should be borne in so stinking a towne as Edinburgh in lousy Scotland ... where they christen without Cross, marry without Ring, receive the Sacrament without Reverence, die without Repentance and bury without Divine Service.*

Thus far Anthony Welden, 'Clerk of the Kitchen' and 'Clerk of the Green Cloth' to James VI (and I), and if he could so lampoon his King's Scottish capital, little wonder that others found our northern hills 'forbidding'. It is, however, reassuring to know that this same Sir Anthony lost his job at Court in 1617 for 'a-satirising of the Scots'.

The eighteenth century continued the tradition of neglect and dismissed the Grampians as 'horrid'. Doubtless, Dr Johnson's notion that the only satisfactory view in Scotland was that of the road to England arose from his characteristic denigration of these mountains whose appearance, said he, was 'that of matter incapable of usefulness, dismissed by nature from her care and disinherited of her favours'. And Captain Burt followed Sam Johnson's lead in his *Letters from a Gentleman in the North of Scotland to a Friend in London*, where he described our hills as 'most of all disagreeable when the heath is in bloom'. This in the reign of George I—but there were probably midges then, as now. The Doctor and his fastidiously discerning eighteenth-century world, including the disgruntled Captain Burt, would have agreed with the Deeside ghillie who warned John Hill Burton a century later that Speyside 'was a fery fulgar place not fit for a young shentleman to be goin' to at all, at all'.

The nineteenth itself was already several decades old before interest in these mountains awoke in earnest. They were neither much explored, not even by the hardy drovers of the Lairig Ghru and the Lairig an Laoigh, nor accurately measured till the Ordnance Survey got to work upon them well on in Victoria's reign. True, Napoleon had done them a service by taking the resorts of Europe out of the reach of the English, and in 1814 George Fennell Robson could say that the 'Highland Scenery of Scotland has received … much attention from the opulent inhabitants of this country, during their exclusion from the Continent…' When Napoleon was no longer there to exclude these opulent folk from their favourite 'continental tours', most of them soon forgot the *ersatz* pleasure of the Scottish hills, which reverted to their obscurity as 'ferry fulgar places'. Nor was it only the Grampians that fell under the general ban, for we find in the 1854 edition of Murray's *Handbook of Switzerland* the statement, too precious to be lost in oblivion, that it is 'a somewhat remarkable fact, that while the ascent of Mont Blanc was attempted by few, a large proportion of those who have made the ascent are persons of unsound mind'.

The earliest recorded place-names on the Cairngorm map were not, as one might suppose, those of the prominent summits but those of islands, rivers and estuaries: in a word, objects near the coast showing the seafarer his landfall, while the hilly hinterland remained almost a *terra incognita*. Only long after the coast was thus made clear did the mountains begin to single themselves out and be named in their turn. Abraham Ortelius, the sixteenth-century map-maker of Antwerp, shows us how it was done. He was Geographer to Philip II of Spain, came to England to draft the map of England and Wales with the Welshman, Humphrey Llwyd, and published in 1570 his own *Theatrum Orbis Terrarum*.

In 1750, Captain Patten of General Guise's Regiment, in reporting the movements of the Highland

Military Patrols after the '45, calls Tummel Bridge 'Kinnachen', and Trinafour 'Innesour', while, to take but once instance among many in our own time, the earlier Ordnance Survey Map marks both the Tullochgrues in Rothiemurchus as 'Balvadden'.

Doubtless the maps of the mid-nineteenth century had improved on Ortelius and Captain Patten but they were still imperfect guides and it is hardly to be wondered that, in his *Cairngorm Mountains* of 1864, John Hill Burton is sometimes astray in the use of names. He calls Lochnagar 'Lochin-ye-gair', and Lochan Uaine 'Loch-na-Youn'. To him, Etchachan is 'Ettichan' and Lynwilg 'Lynvaig'. His map was almost as inexact as the 'plan' that made General Wade call for something more 'exact' that night in the Ruthven Barracks, away back in the time of George II. Most of the names that Hill Burton used had passed from lip to lip for centuries and were only in his own time being put into print. And he throws some light on how it was done in a passage describing his first ascent of Ben Nevis:

Turning my eyes … from the yawning precipice to what I expected to be a solitary mountain-top, I saw nothing more nor less than a crowd of soldiers, occupying nearly the whole tableland of the summit! Yes, there they were, British troops, with their red coats, dark-grey trousers, and fatigue caps, as distinctly as I had ever seen them on the parade-ground of Edinburgh Castle! ... substantial, able-bodied fellows; what could it mean? ... A very short sentence from the good-humoured-looking young fellow who received our first breathless and perplexed inquiry solved the mystery—'Did you never hear of the Ordnance Survey?' To be sure everybody had heard of it; but the impression created concerning it was as of something like a mathematical line, with neither breadth nor thickness; but here it was in substantial operation ... They had already conducted some operations on Ben Muich Dhui, and they were now commencing such surveys on Ben Nevis as would enable them finally to decide which of these mountains has the honour of being the highest land in the United Kingdom. Competition had of late run very close between them; and the last accounts had shown Ben Muich Dhui only some twenty feet or so ahead.

Here we have the testimony of the Scottish historian to the lateness of our knowledge of our own hills, for the occasion of his encounter with the Sappers on the top of Ben Nevis cannot have been as much as a century ago and may well have been later than 1850. His pleasant book was published in 1864 but, as much of it was written before then for occasional publication in Blackwood's Magazine, we may put the verification of Ben Nevis' claim to be the highest in the United Kingdom about the time of the Indian Mutiny and the American Civil War.

But, as we have seen, verification of height is one thing and certainty of nomenclature quite another. Science proves the first but human vagaries in two languages rule the second. Moreover, the variety of the Gaelic is such that the translator must *either* use one and the same English word for several Gaelic turns of phrase, each with a different shade of meaning and many with distinct meanings of their own, *or* devise some adequate conveyance of meaning in paraphrase. This is particularly true of the vocabulary of the mountains, in which the 'mere English' is wholly defeated by the wealth of the Gaelic. In the December 1940 issue of the *Cairngorm Club Journal* (Vol XV, No 81) P A Spalding says:

England being on the whole a level land, the English language is poor in general words descriptive of high and mountainous country. Gaelic, on the other hand, is rich—so rich that it is absolutely impossible to find English equivalents, for a tithe of this verbal wealth. This is sufficient to show that if the men who named the mountains did not feel inclined to go into ecstasies about them, they looked at them closely, and carefully differentiated the types of mountain contour from one another. They had a highly developed sense of mountain form; nor did they lack words to distinguish what they saw.

The strictly accurate translator is thus sometimes astray in conveying the essence of the Gaelic sense, and the more imaginative, though less meticulous, interpreter is usually more faithful to the original meaning. There is, for instance, the sloping shoulder on the north-western flank of Cairn Gorm himself which bears the name Sron an Aonach, which I translate as the Nose-That-Stands-by-Itself. Others have called it the Lonely Shoulder, and so on. But none of these guesses at meaning actually point to the source where the name arises. Sron an Aonach is the Nose, or Promontory, which points towards, or belongs to, Aonach, and Aonach is the name of a round turret of hill below the Sron which stands by itself and is therefore called the One Apart, or the Sole or Single Hill.

Carn a' Mhaim, Devil's Point and the Lairig Ghru

Carn a' Mhaim, to me the Hill of the Unique Reward, also bears a disputed name, one party in the dispute claiming that Mhaim is the pass in which this shapely hill stands, another maintaining that the word is a corruption of Mhain (single or alone), while a third makes the confident claim set out below. Nothing more natural than to call Carn a' Mhaim, standing *in* the Lairig as no other hill does, the Hill of the Pass (and if you look down from your coign of vantage below the Pools of Dee you will see how Carn a' Mhaim and Bod an Diabholl, the Devil's Point, are the doorposts of the eastern gateway to the Pass)— but nothing farther from the truth, nonetheless.

I will confess that, till a moment about twelve years ago, I had only given this Hill of the Pass a *proxime accessit* in the Honours List of the Cairngorms. I had liked its contours, found something satisfying in its shape, noted the colour of wine in its shaded side, talked of its 'difference' from many other hills and, in a word, given it due credit for its part in the grand panorama. But, till the moment mentioned above, I had not given Carn a' Mhaim the accolade 'Hill of the Unique Reward'. In all my previous sights of this lesser hill on the Aberdeenshire side of the Cairngorms, and they were many, I was being apprenticed, as it were, for the chosen moment when, as we came out to the edge of the steep drop into the bed of the Dee below, my daughter Joan said, 'But, Dad, she's the loveliest of them all.'

A double stroke of genius there! Not only to single out Carn a' Mhaim for her beauty but to give her the quality of difference that I had always missed. I had not seen why this Hill of the Pass stood alone in a glory of her own. You may see this, or you may not. You may remind me that 'Carn' is masculine in the Gaelic and that all who bear the title must be males. But that is just where Carn a' Mhaim breaks and proves the rule. I shall not try to persuade the unpersuadable. I am content to share with Joan a monopoly of devotion to the Queen of the Cairngorms, almost in the hope that no one else will come forward to make the same confession of delight in her and thus infringe our copyright. From that moment when Joan seized my arm on the edge beyond the Soldier's Corrie, Carn a' Mhaim became the 'lass unparalleled'.

For she takes her name, not from her place but from her quality. Her Gaelic name means the Hill of the Shapely Lines—Mhaim being one of the score of words describing the hills in all their shapes and moods. Its literal sense is a swelling, its second sense, a rounded gently rising hill, and its particular title is the Hill of the Shapely Lines or, if you will, the Girl with a Good Figure.

It is high time to look at the Cairngorms themselves. And if beauty be indeed in the eye of the beholder, the picture of these mountains must be somewhat individual, personal to the beholder who attempts to make it. Others will find much in it that is familiar, if sometimes something that is strange. And since we find in Carn a' Mhaim or in Loch Avon what we bring to it, many readers will say to themselves, 'But that isn't how I see it at all.' Granted, but that proves, not the faulty or oblique vision of one beholder, but the quality of universality which is in the Cairngorms.

It also shows how much the impression owes to the moment of its making: to storm and calm, to light and shade, and to all those fleeting, changing, baffling gleams and shadows that pass across the face of this range at all seasons of the year. Moreover, the point of departure decides the setting of the picture, bringing each feature into sight and focus from a different angle of vision. The walker from Coylum Bridge starts from his Rothiemurchus outlook, the stalker taking the Foxhunter's Path from Achlean to the shoulder of Carn Ban has his own perspective, the visitor approaching through the Slugan Pass sees a panorama of his own in turn, while the Deeside Aberdonian comes at the whole range, as it were, from the other side of the world.

Two
Cairn Gorm

For the distant sight of the Cairngorms, there will be many claimants to the first place among coigns of vantage. Morrone of Deeside comes high in the list. It stands back from the panorama in an apex of its own, with the little stream of Cluny on one side and the dip to Inverey in the foreground, beyond which the eye travels up Glen Lui to Derry Cairngorm and Ben Macdhui, with the steep eastern wall of the whole range presenting a sharper face than anything to be seen from the Spey. But Morrone is just a little too far from the scene to claim first priority. The eleven-mile distance from it to the summit of Ben Macdhui somewhat flattens the whole perspective. The rival stance, also at a range of eleven miles, might once have been found at Aviemore's Loch Vaa, although the Herdsman blocks the left side of the picture. From the steep bank among the stunted birches above that little sheet of water, with its shores spread below you like the outline of a continent in miniature and the moorhen rising and diving in silence, leaving a spreading ring on the smooth water, the Cairngorms still fill the horizon in an almost perfect frame. But, in forty years, the birches have grown and raised a screen which almost obscures the whole view.

Some will claim that better still is the sudden view of them, at a longer range of fourteen miles, from the Carrbridge road after the railway cutting at Slochd is left behind and the watershed of the Monadh Liath mountains is overpast on the way to Aviemore. And, by the same token, the terrace of the Aviemore Hotel has no mean outlook, though I think it is well beaten by other stances, say at the turn of the Loch Morlich road about half-way between the Loch and Coylum Bridge, where a mound of heather invites the passer-by to sit and take his fill of beauty.

Such are the set pieces, the panoramas known to all. But there are quick glimpses that stay more intimately in the memory. Pause for a moment on the Spey Bridge at Insh, to see the Corrie Lochan summit of Braeriach set in the angle where the skyline of Creag Mh'geachaidh meets the Sgoran Dubh range above Allt Mharcaidh—making a finished picture in a perfect frame, though itself no more than a glimpse. Here Braeriach is not a broad waste of gravel and boulder but a crest of character sharply etched in light and shadow. But these are only halts on the road for the sightseer. The mountains themselves ask for closer acquaintance and the varying approaches to them give the key to the picture which each lover of them will carry in his memory.

Let us bring Cairn Gorm himself to the test of these contrasted approaches. No one has ever dared to claim that the mountain which gives his name to the whole range fully deserves the honour. Some indeed, and I among them, will call him dull and in a moment I shall confess my autobiographical reason

Loch Insh

for saying so: a dull hill and a dreary climb. A waggish fellow-climber once said, in an out-of-breath pause below the Marquis Well, that Cairn Gorm 'gave up trying once he had stolen copyright in the title of these hills ... that he never put his best foot forward because he hadn't one to put.'

Well, it's an ill job being smart at the expense of anyone so imperturbable as Cairn Gorm and this *ex cathedra* verdict (the speaker was a cleric) has no sooner been pronounced than the voice of Loch Avon is heard in challenge, in a well-taken protest. That long dark loch has a right to speak. For, whatever may be the *longueurs* of Cairn Gorm's north-western slopes, however prosaic and interminable may be the toil of the climber from Loch Morlich, the scene changes on Cairn Gorm's eastern side. Look at him from almost any point you please above the south-east shore of Loch Avon, through the gap at the farther end of Loch Etchachan, with the deep cleft of Glen Avon beyond, and you will have reason to doubt the truth of my clerical friend.

Here, then, Cairn Gorm has a best foot and puts it forward well. From these points of vantage, he justifies the old Aberdonian gibe that those who approach Cairn Gorm from Rothiemurchus or by the Ryvoan (or Rebhoan) Pass have only seen his back door. (I think the Aberdonian actually said his backside.) A jewel has many facets and its beauty is not to be found in the setting fashioned by the jeweller but in its own planes and jutting edges that take the light. Cairn Gorm's north-western flank is but the setting that holds him to earth. Elsewhere he rises and soars like some of his fellows in the range, and on at least two sides he takes the morning and the evening light in such fashion as to reveal him the worthy partner—some would say the *primus inter pares*—of his great Grampian neighbours. I am not among the some who say that, but I enter here their not ill-founded claim.

I made my first acquaintance with Cairn Gorm some fifty years ago when I was a small boy. A mixed party set out to climb the mountain, though indeed 'climb' is too heroic a word for that tedious promenade. We drove in wagonettes—the word must be almost as archaic now as the vehicle itself—from the smithy in the Rothiemurchus triangle at Inverdruie. The drive by Coylum Bridge and the pockmarked moor road to Loch Morlich was a memorable beginning of a Red Letter Day for me, for the coachman let me have his whip but cramped my style a little by his warning, 'Noo, master Fred, ye mun ca' canny wi' the whup. Thae beasts dinna need the lash.'

Once on the mountain, I ran like a stag for a spell but soon lost my first wind and never got my second, so that by the time we reached the rock (which I was then told was the Shelter Stone, which it wasn't, but maybe it was Clach Bharraig) I had little ambition to finish the climb and jumped at the chance of playing The Robbers' Cave round the big boulder, instead of going on to the top. The Robber Chief was William Peyton of Broughty Ferry, by profession a Free Church minister, but by zeal a student of the rocks and by nature a lover of the Cairngorms.

I sometimes wonder whether I should ever have gained my feeling for the Cairngorms if Peyton had not planted the seed fifty years ago. I well remember him saying, 'They aren't just things to climb, mountains to say you've been to the top of. Anyone can do that, but some day you'll find they're almost like people you can get to know.' After fifty years, I may not quote his very words but the notion behind them took root and now flowers in this endeavour to show that he was right when he said that they were 'like people you can get to know'. And, maybe, I kept Peyton's words the more firmly in my mind because, unlike most grown-ups, he could play the fool or the robber chief to admiration, and then turn round and talk like an equal to a little chap staggering over the rough ground at his side. For Peyton knew the golden rule that you can never talk down to your audience, whether they are a small boy or the General Assembly of the Free Church of Scotland.

He was a frequent and welcome guest in my father's house, especially as a holiday companion, and his deeply tanned face and piercing but kindly eyes were as familiar to the children as to the elders. I must have guessed by instinct what was afterwards written about him, that his mind 'showed a union of science and mysticism, fused in the crucible of a flowing and scintillating imagination—a union too rare to bring popular recognition to the writer, but profoundly stimulating to the minds of his friends.' He himself wrote to my father, 'I have an idea that scientific conceptions' (he was no mean geologist) 'can be translated into the poetic and the philosophic, and that they have been anticipated by the poet and the philosopher.'

Peyton's name has long since faded in the back pages of Scottish Church history, and even there will be hard to find, but it has never faded from my memory. The Robbers' Cave, played in a Cairn Gorm mist, with William Peyton as Robber Baron, was a thing to remember, and has been remembered. But just where this romance of childhood was played I cannot fix. More than once have I tried to reconstruct the scene, some saying that it must have been at the Marquis Well and others placing it under this or that great stone on the north-western shoulder of Cairn Gorm. We glanced at Clach Bharraig as the possible scene a moment ago, but wherever and whenever I have gone to look for it, the cave had so shrunk with time that it was no longer its old self, or had vanished altogether. Better not to seek it on the map, for one of the feats beyond the powers of His Majesty's Ordnance Survey is to reconstruct the dramatic geography of childhood. Nonetheless, the Cave and William Peyton the Robber Chief are safe and real in the Never Never Land of memory and they will always be the secret of Cairn Gorm to me.

And here, perhaps, is the source of my disappointment with the mountain that gives his name to the whole range. Not only is his Inverness-shire flank a long slope of little character but, having failed to hold the magic of my first moments with him, he has never recovered his first reputation and never will, as far as I am concerned. Cairn Gorm is thus unfairly handicapped in the race with his fellows, but how much does he care?

Part of the claim made by the Counsel for the Defence of Cairn Gorm is derived, not from what he looks like but what he looks at. And even the most crabbed of Cairn Gorm's detractors cannot cavil at the view from the top. He has the advantage of standing somewhat apart from his three towering associates and, even at the risk of being led astray into comparisons, we may remember in his favour that his view of the other heights is almost better than their varying outlook upon him and upon themselves, while from west right round by the north and down to the south-east no one gets in his way. By contrast, Ben Macdhui cannot see over the peaks of the matchless Braeriach–Carn Toul massif, and they in turn sometimes find him in the way. But only the distant view is thus in any way obstructed by any of the foursome and if, by the weakness of human nature, we yield to the temptation to put our money on any one of the four as prince of the nearer view, maybe Carn Toul… But we shall see, and we have not reached him yet!

The spreading scene from the summit of Cairn Gorm tempts the watcher to linger. It may not have the advantage of some more isolated Scottish peaks of being able to see from sea to sea, but comes very near it. I have heard it said that the front seat in the stalls for those who seek the wide horizon-sweep is the Cuillins in Skye, and I will myself put in a claim for Aberdeenshire's Morrone, for Skye's Beinn-na-Cailleach, for Perthshire's Schiehallion, or for even lower hills who can see the bigger ones as they cannot see themselves. And, as Caleb George Cash has proved in his twopenny indicator, the top of the water-tank at Aviemore station has advantages of accessibility and panoramic sweep often denied to more exalted watchtowers. There must be some, not many perhaps, for it is now long ago, who will remember the tall figure of this teacher of geography, with the long black beard and Norfolk jacket, seated on a camp stool on the south-going platform of the station, checking the perspective with pencil held at arm's length as he drew the panorama of the Cairngorms that you can still buy at the store which I cannot help calling Lawrence's, but which has since become the 'co-op shop'.

But we have not come to the cairn of Cairn Gorm merely to wish ourselves down again on the banks of the Spey. Here we can see the coloured counties spread before us to the Moray Firth and leagues beyond, with horizons wider far than any you can see from Bredon. And of all the coloured counties, the foreground of Glen More, with the silver, blue and gold of Loch Morlich set in the dark forest green, and the valley of the Spey beyond it, give Cairn Gorm's panorama variety and expanse at least as great as most of his neighbours enjoy. Ben Rinnes stands out, and the white finger of Tarbat Ness Lighthouse and, on the western skyline, a whole phalanx of mountains.

I once asked a French visitor what stood out in his mind in recollection of the Cairn Gorm view.

'Mais rien: je ne retiens rien que l'ensemble. Mais quel ensemble!'

A point well taken.

I ought perhaps to add that my French friend had no interest whatever in the map and found us a little ridiculous in our lively dispute whether the little sandheap due north of us was, or was not, Morven-above-Helmsdale, and whether the sharp little triangle on the horizon filling a tiny gap to the left of Ben Wyvis was, or was not, Ben Dearg, or perhaps the little brother of Ben Wyvis who stands beside him to the south-west. And while the familiar wrangle went on—'Of course you can't see Little Ben Wyvis, the

Monadh Liaths come in between'—it was accompanied by an obligato of Gallic epithets, with pauses of enraptured silence, in which the Frenchman paid his tribute to the ensemble. Cairn Gorm had found a good witness for the defence in him.

Three
Four Peaks Circuit

Forty years ago, a party of three climbed Cairn Gorm twice in twelve hours and made the circuit of the whole ring of the Monadh Ruadh before returning home again. It was near midsummer and neither stalker nor gamekeeper put any obstacle in our way, so we resolved to 'do' all four summits, and some others, in the course of one outing.

We left the larger and lazier part of a picnic company on the golden sands of Loch Morlich, near the point chosen by the photographer for the picture that later adorned the cover of the one-inch Ordnance Survey map of the Cairngorms, and set out with full rucksacks across the flat ground at the eastern end of the loch. As we crossed the footbridge, with the sun already well down in the western sky, Hugh Miller said, 'Funny ideas they had about Cairn Gorm. I read somewhere that one of the first men to describe the Cairngorms—'

'Old Pont, probably.'

'Hardly. Pont didn't know Cairn Gorm. He only

saw the hill from away down the Deeside.'

'Dunno that, but he said Cairn Gorm was *four miles high!* What's four miles? Twenty thousand feet, about. Glad we haven't to do all *that* before sunset.'

'But, that's just what we have to do,' said I. 'And what your old Johnny meant was that it was a four-mile climb to the top. And it's four miles as the crow flies, as near as makes no matter, from this very bridge to the top. So Pont, or whoever it was, wasn't quite the BF you thought.'

'How long will it take us?'

'Peyton's rule was three miles to the hour, and half an hour to add for every thousand feet up—which makes, allowing us a bit of a wander off the crow-flight line, something about three hours. But today we'll do it in less. Let's see: it's not quite six now and the sun sets at a bit after nine. We'll be up there with half an hour to spare before sunset, but we'll have to keep going to do it.'

And we kept going, at a fast pace, in an uneventful climb over Sron an Aonach—the Nose-That-Stands-By-Itself—to the Marquis Well, Fuaran a' Mharcuis, with never a sign all the way to show where my Robber Cave had been. A halt at the Well, with rucksacks off and pipes alight and the first of many roving talks about how the corries and peaks of the High Cairngorms got their names. But I was impatient to lose no moment of the midsummer sunset from the cairn, and so we quickly covered the last hundred feet to the summit, where the hunt for the origin of names had free play while we watched the lovely setting of the summer sun beyond the hills of the west. Where, for instance, was the Cattle Corrie that gave its name to the shoulder just north of us, Cnap Coire na Spreidhe? And when did cattle graze at this height? There is no hollow deep enough to be called a corrie anywhere round the Cnap itself and our question has probably been asked many a time and never answered. The Marquis Well is the source of the Allt na Ciste, the burn which flows through the corrie of that name, and the Ciste itself is supposed to be Margaret's coffin.

But the blaze of sunset glory along the north-western horizon silences all dispute, for here the first object of our outing is in sight. No doubt the frequenters of the High Cairngorms will never settle the question whether the first or the last hour of the day is the better, and so, as long as there are hills to climb and men to climb them, the matter will be taken to avizandum and never a verdict pronounced. Nor would

I ask for anything better than a battle of wits over the rival merits of the Rising and the Setting Sun. George Meredith's Diana would have it that 'prose can paint evening and moonlight, but poets are needed to sing the dawn'. Maybe. Nonetheless I took *my* side long ago, the partisan of Nightfall in the Hills.

Already, in the deep shaft of Loch A'an behind us, the gloom is settling on the smooth water out of sight, while the valleys before us lie like shadows below the heights still tipped with light. And after the red disc of the sun sinks, the last edge of his fiery rim dropping beneath the horizon, suddenly, almost with an audible click, he leaves behind him such a train of colour that one may see what the Shropshire Lad saw when he watched the sunset bleeding on the road to Wales. The sky changes. No longer is it the amphitheatre of space through which the sun moves on his daily course. It becomes an ocean, stretching leagues beyond the sunset bar, with long clouds like islands set in a vast expanse of slowly darkening sea.

There is a chill in the air which prompts us to move. Light there is still, for the midsummer night is never dark in these northern hills, but if we are to keep warm during the waiting hours down below at the Shelter Stone we must make our own warmth in movement. So we set off from the cairn, half resolved to return to watch the sunrise from the same coign of vantage. On our way to the invisible line which divides Cairn Gorm from Ben Macdhui, we pass the black rocks which Peyton taught me to call the Knuckles, peer over the edge of the Snowy Corrie (Coire an t'Sneachda), stop for a moment to look at the rim of Cairn Lochan etched against the pale western sky and thence stride across the wide plateau to the Tawny Burn, with a broad bed of snow in the hollows.

When we first come to the edge of the corrie where this same Feith Buidhe—the Yellow-Watercourse-that-comes-out-of-the-Bog—falls down to the head of Loch A'an, we see more clearly than ever the wonderful shaded colours of the loch itself, for though it is in gloom it is still not colourless. In this colouring, it is sharply contrasted with Loch Einich on the other massif of the Cairngorms. Einich is dark and almost uniform in its peaty colour, with only a splash of brighter tint at its upper and lower end—or so I have always seen it though, to be sure, much depends on the light thrown on it. Loch Avon has greater variety of colour and shares with Carn a' Mhaim a flavour of claret, too indeterminate to be called purple, too cloudy to be called violet, yet somewhere in the spectrum near indigo, with an olive-green shadow shot through it. It looks like a dark velvet carpet, spread between the frowning cliffs of Beinn Mheadhoin in the south and the steep rockfall of Stac na Faraidh and the Saddle on the Cairn Gorm side of the loch. The fringe of the carpet is embroidered with pale green where the yellow sand of the shallowing shore brightens the dark water.

We stayed for a while to watch the colour slowly fade and the central depth of the loch grow ever darker till it was almost black. And in the last moments of the gloaming, having made a detour across the patches of snow round the corrie at the head of Loch Avon, we came out to the edge of the Shelter Stone Crag, with the loch five hundred feet beneath and the steep side of Cairn Gorm across the loch, leading up through Corrie Robert to the summit beyond. We looked across to the great bird in flight, shaped like the Isle of Skye, that is sculptured on the shoulder above the corrie. The pale design of his outspread wings showed clear against the darker surrounding slope even in the gathering twilight, while in the gloom of the loch below nothing was distinguishable except the faint thin line upon the shore where land and water met.

Turning back from the high edge of the Crag, we found a bed of hard snow in the steep gully between it and Cairn Etchachan and glissaded down the funnel (slithered is the fitter word for our descent) for two or three hundred feet, till the boulders among the loose wet snow below forced us to work our way to the edge and to scramble more slowly down among the stones and scree that lie like a flounced apron round the bottom of the Crag. We did not pause to give the Slithering Gully a name, but I believe that a month later (viz July 1904) another party of climbers called it the Castle Gates Gully. Doubtless they noted some feature which prompted this title and, moreover, we were using it as a toboggan slide from above, whereas they would see it in more dignified guise from below as a stiffish climb, with the walls of the gully at the top looking like the gates of a castle. On *my* Ordnance Survey map it bears the name Slithering Gully in red ink.

On the way down, Hugh had passed me as his feet slipped from under him and he changed from a standing to a sitting glissade, shouting, 'We ride on the pants triumphing.'

A few minutes later, when we traversed the flounce of loose debris under the Crag, I said to him, 'What was that you shouted as you passed me up there?'

'Oh, a bit of Antony.'

'Antony what?'

'A not unknown play by William Shakespeare, Freddie.'

Hugh's natural burr sounded more burry and reproachful than usual. But that was his way. He would never cap a quotation with any obvious verse but with something aptly unusual. A little earlier in the evening, McGilky said he knew there were lots of bits of poetry one ought to quote up here but he never could remember them at the right moment. In that, McGilky was like the rest of us but Hugh quoted Alice's words at him:

'I can repeat poetry as well as other folk, if it comes to that—'

'Oh, it needn't come to that!' said Alice hastily.

'It often comes to that with *you*,' I said.

'I dunno,' said Hugh. 'I couldn't quote you the Lord's Prayer and get the petitions in the right order, or even 'Mary had a little lamb', to save my life, but the other things always stick in my head.'

'They would,' said McGilky.

So we came down the steep Etchachan flank of Loch A'an to the Stone of Shelter, Clach Dhean, a little to the south-west of the head of the loch. The night of midsummer had already fallen, and with it a sudden coldness which made us take the sweaters from our knapsacks to keep out the chill. The last light of day was dying out of the western sky over the High Cairngorms but the summer night never grew completely dark, except in the deep shadow of Glen Avon. There is a luminous canopy above, even at the darkest hour below. In the far north, the midnight sun seems to prove that light is never extinguished, but here, at midnight and in the first hours of the following day, there is neither utter darkness nor anything but a pale reflection of midsummer's midnight light. He who has watched this setting of the sun, which is never followed by unrelieved darkness, feels himself surrounded by a continuous uncertain twilight, which links the sunset and the dawn. And, unless he hides himself in some deep corner of shadow, he will hardly know when sunset ends and dawn begins. Nor, indeed, has he seen dawn itself who has not seen the night never fade into darkness round the northern rim of the world and day return again by stealth across the distant coast of Banff.

But for us, in the deep cleft of Loch A'an, there was an interlude of something like real darkness as we settled down for a few hours at the Shelter Stone to await the dawn. The Stone of Shelter is exactly what its name implies. It is a great boulder, fifteen hundred tons in weight and five times the height of a man, a mountain in miniature with a flat base resting on supporting stones which raise it above the slope on which it stands. Whether it fell off the rockface of its own splendid crag above, or whether the glacier long ago left it behind because it was too heavy to carry, I must leave to the geologists to decide. There are other great stones in other parts of the range not unlike this Shelter, and there is one lower down Loch Avon which John Hill Burton describes as 'a stone about the size of a Parish Church lying like a pebble at the foot of the mountain, with a projecting ledge on the lee side sufficiently large to protect our party'.

Well, parish church or not, *our* Stone of Shelter is but a good-sized hut and whichever may win the competition in size, none of them is better poised like a roof for the protection of the night-farer in the Cairngorms than this well-named Shelter Stone. It is the Half Way House and Wayside Inn for those who may need a halting place in their way across these hills, but it is not quite so accessible as the taverns of the plains and you will not take your ease at your

The Shelter Stone

inn in any kind of luxury under its roof. There are bundles of dry heather on the stone floor on which men can sleep and it is reported that one party made it their home for over a week. Most of its tenants stay but a few hours between midnight and dawn.

We paced the stone from end to end, a very 'rough' measurement in both senses, and found it between fifteen and sixteen full paces long, say between forty-five and fifty feet. Inside, it is a low-roofed chamber like the Abbot's cell at Clairvaux, so built that he could not stand upright nor stretch himself upon his bed—this the discipline that Bernard de Clairvaux must undergo as a nightly reminder that here we have no continuing city. At the Shelter Stone, self-discipline or no, we have no continuing city, only a memorable halt by the Cairngorm wayside. So low is it that at the entrance facing the loch you must stop and crawl, and just high enough towards the back to allow a short man to stand almost upright. I hit my head on the roof several times and so proved that its highest point is well under six feet. It is not completely watertight, but successive tenants during the past half-century have paid their rent in service by packing stones and moss to fill the gaps round the bottom, thus keeping it bone-dry but leaving plenty of elbow-room for draughts to play round the occupants, and as these draughts, even in high summer, come off the snow-wreaths in the gullies and corries above, the air is not warm.

Since those days of forty years ago, the Shelter Stone has undergone certain improvements by the addition of sundry 'tenants' fixtures', including a Visitors' Book placed in a tin box by the Cairngorm Club of Aberdeen. A pity it wasn't there from the beginning! It would have been interesting to have proof that 'eighteen armed men' found refuge there in the eighteenth century, especially if they had left their impressions of the accommodation provided, because in modern times it is reckoned that half that number would make a crowd at the Shelter Stone. But, book or no book, many of those early visitors, being outlaws and freebooters, would have left no trace of themselves when they departed, preferring to cover their tracks against all pursuers.

We had seen the sun go down in the west from the top of Cairn Gorm and, discussing the matter on our way round the corrie, we had left it to the toss of a coin to decide where to go to watch him rise again. We were well accoutred for a night in the open and, on arriving at the Stone, we found that its last tenants had paid their rent by leaving a slab of chocolate, a packet of Woodbines and an empty half-bottle of Johnnie Walker—not, mark you, a half-empty bottle—all wrapped in packing paper that bore the half-obliterated name 'Bon Accord…' So we knew that our predecessors came from the Granite City. The empty bottle was apostrophised by one of the party, 'Ho, ho! A scurvy legacy indeed!'

It is the unwritten and never-broken law of the Shelter Stone that you shall pay for your keep and so, after eating *their* chocolate and smoking *their* Woodbines, we paid *our* rent by leaving a box of a dozen of John Cotton's 'Edinburgh', an apple and just enough whisky in the half-bottle to tantalise those who came after. But that was done in the darkest hour before dawn and we had still time to spend before setting out again. None of us thought of sleep. We thanked our stars that the night was fine; we talked of 'shoes and sealing wax and whether pigs had wings'. McGilky went down to Loch Avon to boast that he had bathed in it at one in the morning, and Hugh and I followed him to prove that he shirked the shock—which he did.

On our return to the Stone, Hugh took a stump of candle and a slip of paper out of his pocket.

'Did you know,' said he, with the air of ascending the rostrum to instruct a class, 'that "Scotland is … a dissected table land … of extremely complex geological structure?"'

'Come off it,' we said.

He did not come off it but continued.

'I knew we'd need something to while away the time, so I brought a bit of Tarr for you to chew.'

'Tar?'

'No. The Prof. And here's what he says:
Wherever in the Highlands the ice spread out, and hence became ineffective in erosion, one sees the normal conditions of a maturely dissected

land-surface—normal divides, accordant tributaries, irregularities due to sub-aerial denudation and even disintegrated rock. Wherever one enters a trough along which he has reason to expect that ice currents moved vigorously, he finds topographic forms normal to ice work, and common in, and confined to, regions where glaciers have been, but utterly out of harmony with the known results of river denudation—steepened valley walls, truncated spurs, hanging valleys, erased tributaries, lowered cols, and through valleys.

The reading of this extract from professional punditry was punctuated, but not punctured by, a fire of interruptions, and Hugh went on.

'It'll enliven you to know that we are now on "a plane of denudation", also called a peneplain—not tuppence-coloured, mind you.'

'It doesn't need a geologist to tell us that, with these bare hills round us an' all.'

'And somewhere he calls them monadnocks. Why?'

'Dunno, but it may be the Gaelic for naked or for night. So why not the "Mountains of the Naked Night"? Looks like that tonight, anyway!'

So Hugh had his way and we were launched on

a geological debate, with less than the average roadmender's knowledge of stones between us, though, to be sure, Hugh had real mason's heredity in him, for he was the grandson of Hugh Miller of *The Witness* and *Old Red Sandstone*. Even so, our Hugh had not followed faithfully in his ancestor's footsteps, except in his taste for good writing. Nor did we have with us the Geological Survey's map, otherwise we might have talked more sense.

At last McGilky said sleepily, 'The geologists are pretty near as bad as the astronomers at making you feel dizzy.'

'They don't make me feel that way at all. Their names for the rocks sound quite friendly, like soccer teams. I like to think of the Adrishaig Phyllites playing the Pitlochry Grits, with the Tayvallich Conglomerates (sounds like a scratch team in a Saturday afternoon pick-up game) drawn for a bye in the Dalradian championship. And when it comes to the Blair Atholl Series, the Perthshire Green Beds seem to have it all their own way.'

'That,' said Hugh, 'is an unpardonable and bewildering digression.'

'Hear the degenerate descendant of *Old Red Sandstone* deny the faith of his only decent ancestor. I'm talking perfectly sound (or maybe unsound) geology,' retorted I.

'Come off it, both of you,' said McGilky. 'Geology or no geology, Cairn Gorm'll still be there tomorrow morning. No, this morning, and the sun will be there before us if we don't soon get a move on.'

'It's still as dark as ever, if you call it dark, down there.' And looking up, Hugh fell to quoting Meredith, declaiming 'Lucifer in Starlight' in resounding tones that broke the stillness. From the cliff wall opposite round to the corrie's head, the echo sounded sonorous, longer, eerie, in the starry silent night.

And it still was the darkest hour before the dawn. Even the snowfield filling the bowl above us to the left could hardly find a glimmer to cast upwards from its reflector surface and the last faint shadow of light had faded from the unrippled face of Loch Avon and the erect mass of the Shelter Stone Crag looked more like a great tree stump than ever. Darkness itself seemed visible under the shadow of the great hills, for 'the shaft of darkness has its lustre too'. This is the moment when space contracts and all distance is foreshortened, and one can say with Hotspur

... it were an easy leap
To pluck bright honour from the pale-fac'd moon.

To be sure, it is no rhetoric like Hotspur's that the scene inspires. And, to be sure again, there is no moon. Neither breath nor movement breaks the spell. The distant train in the valley, and the whaup crying down below, only serve to deepen by their passing sound the night's enfolding calm.

But there is already a change, the herald of the coming day, and the first faint glow of 'dawn leans across the dark sea'. One could suppose that the nameless tenth-century poet who wrote these words (Englished for us from the mediaeval Latin by Helen Waddell) had stood on the shore of Loch Avon when Dawn's Left Hand was in the sky, watching the shadows change and steal away, come and go upon the unruffled shimmering surface, marking how light can grow when dawn first leans across that dark sea.

(ii)

Reversing the principle *qui dort, dine,* and as none of us slept, we had our first meal of the day just before setting out: a lunch-at-midnight of an oatcake-and-cheese sandwich, a handful of currants and a bar of chocolate, which, though we had never heard of the science of diet, was as well designed a meal as the most modern dietician could prescribe. The hard-boiled eggs and meat sandwiches (including the Herring Bap*) were kept for a later stage in the long day before us, and we drank nothing till we were on the top of Cairn Gorm waiting for the sun to rise. I learned long afterwards from old Parliamentary hands that you can face an all-night sitting of the House of Commons with equanimity if you treat the night as the day. Dinner at eight takes the place of breakfast in this upside-down timetable. Between one and two in the morning, a solid meal is the lunch of the wee sma' hours … 'Never,' said the old hand at the game, 'Never try to get through an all-night sitting on a nibble of biscuit at two in the morning; sit down to a square meal and you'll be all right next day.' And what's true of the House is doubly true of the Hills.

So our Loch A'an picnic at one in the morning set us in good fettle for the day. As we ate in the cold quiet gloom of the threshold of the Shelter Stone, in the great stillness of the summer night, we tossed the coin which sent us back to the summit of Cairn Gorm and then began to forecast our course over the hills, with eighteen hours to spend before the sun would set again. It was to take us to the four main

*See Appendix One

tops, with visits to lesser heights between, and, with luck and weather and good sense, there was no reason why we should not stay the course with ease to the end and return to the Rothiemurchus Triangle long before dark. The final survey of the route and the making of the timetable were left to the moment of the first real halt on the summit of Cairn Gorm while we should wait for the sun to appear somewhere beyond Portsoy.

And so we set out, leaving the rent for our night's lodging in a packet inside the cavern of the Shelter Stone. Sunrise will be soon after three o'clock, perhaps earlier, for at the top of Cairn Gorm the actual rising of the sun will be visible some time before it is due to be seen at Aberdeen, four thousand feet below, and the Aberdeen hour is 3.25 am. The time actually spent at the Shelter Stone that night in June 1904 was well under three hours. We decided to strike straight for Cairn Gorm by the Robert Corrie (Coire Raibeirt), reckoning that we should gain time, even if the corrie were steep (which it is), compared with the detour above the head of Loch Avon by Garbh Uisge and Feith Buidhe once more. As the crow flies, the summit of Cairn Gorm is somewhat under two miles from the Shelter Stone but our course, via the

Robert Corrie, was reckoned as nearer three, with something like 1,700 feet to climb. By the William Peyton 'Rule of Thumb for Climbers', which he had given me ten years before, we ought to have given ourselves one hour and fifty minutes, but as his rule allowed for stoppages to eat, drink or rest, we gave ourselves eighty minutes and actually reached the top in seventy, at 2.25 am. Peyton's Rule of Thumb, as said earlier, gives a *pace* of three miles an hour, with thirty minutes added for every thousand feet. This, I have since learned, is exactly the Naismith Formula, and whether Peyton and Naismith arrived at it independently is no matter, for it tallies with common experience. It is, of course, a rule of averages applicable to long outings and has little bearing on a short spurt such as our early morning climb from the Shelter Stone.

We crossed the burn, Garbh Uisge, by the Milkmaid's Finger at the head of Loch Avon at 1.05 am, made our way diagonally up the steep north-western slope, crossing the Allt na Coire Raibeirt well below the steepest part of the corrie, for we remembered that the going was better on its left bank. We made such good time that we could pause for breath at the 3,250-foot contour and turn to look back at Loch

Avon and its great walls of rock. To the right, the massive square-topped pillar of the Shelter Stone Crag, separated from the sharper peak of Cairn Etchachan by the funnel of our Slithering Gully and looking much less jagged from here than it did from below; opposite us, the flatter top of Beinn Mheadhoin, the Middle Mount, with his row of black tors stark on the faintly lighted horizon, and below us, the dark loch now beginning to recapture some of the colours seen earlier in the night. And soon after resuming our way, we passed close to Cairn Gorm's own protruding black rocks, the Knuckles, once more.

At no hour of the twenty-four are these hills more impressive than in the moment before dawn. The illusion of distance, so well-known to all climbers, is greater than ever. The nearer landscape seems closer than it really is, the middle distance has a most deceiving perspective and the farther horizon loses itself in space not to be measured in miles. There are fewer landmarks by which to reckon distance and the ground underfoot has a uniform colour of grey, deepening as it recedes into a luminous gloom which one rarely sees below the heather or tree line.

We came to the summit of Cairn Gorm as the first light spread round the eastern horizon. The Greater

Light to rule the day was on his way up the slope of dawn. But a low dark barrier of fog lay on the sea beyond Aberdeen and only in the north-east and the south-east was the sky clear down to the horizon, so that somewhere out in the North Sea over the coast of Banff was the only open path of sunrise. And along that path came the first bright light many minutes before the Sun himself rose over the bank of cloud.

Once more, in the fresh clear light of a new day, the wide ensemble of the Cairn Gorm panorama is spread below us. Even distant points stand unusually clear on the horizon of morning and one can believe that the Lochnagar Indicator is telling the truth when it says that from Cac Carn Beag you can—and, if lucky, will—see both the Cheviots on one side and Ben More Assynt on the other. When I stood on that Lochnagar summit forty years ago, a year before the outing now described, I saw no such 'wide orb o' the world', for the northern horizon was closed by cloud over the firth and the southern was a mountain haze over Mearns. But the wider view is there all the time, if often hidden, and thus on Cairn Gorm, or on its majestic rival above Braemar, you stand in the middle of a great circle, with a radius of close on one hundred miles and something not far from one hundred objects on the circumference. Or, taking the view the other way round, you may see (or, at all events, Caleb George Cash has asserted that you can see) the edge of Lochnagar's Cac Carn Beag from Arthur's Seat. At Coylum Bridge in 1901, Cash showed me the bearings he had taken from Arthur's Seat from which he had in mind to design an Arthurian Indicator, and even then his incomplete list of visible tops was nearly fifty, some twenty of them north of the Forth, with Lochnagar the most distant at 68½ miles—the bearing being almost due north 'over the [then] new extension of the docks at Leith'.

This morning we are likely to remain long, too long perhaps, gazing through Zeiss towards the south-east in the endeavour to decide who has lost or won the bet that 'the cone down there beyond is North Berwick Law.' I am sure that it isn't and I put my money, at no more than perhaps even odds, on Largo Law in Fife, not being sanguine even about him, though no more than sixpence is at stake. Visibility is not at its maximum and there is no Indicator here to check our casual observation. Of the identity of other peaks there is no doubt. All the Grampian outposts to the east and the north-east are plainly visible: Mount Keen, Bennachie whose unique 'Knuckle' stands like a wart on the lens of the field-glasses, Ben Rinnes and, farther round to the west, the northern slopes of the Monadh Liath looking greyer than ever under the slanting morning light. On the more distant horizon, the heights of Ross and Caithness and Sutherland seem to be flattened against one another in a grey serrated line on which it is difficult to place the individual peaks, while the farthest points—Ben More Assynt, Ben Hope and Ben Hee—are invisible.

In the middle foreground, almost in line with the Tarbat Ness Light and Morven-in-Helmsdale, the

Loch Avon and the Shelter Stone Crag

unique Culbin Sands of the Moray Firth draw their line of pale chrome turning to gold in the growing light. Even at the distance of forty miles we can see how widely they are spread along the Moray coast westwards from the left bank of the estuary of the Findhorn, while the lesser dunes of the Maviston Sands prolong the gilded line into the county of Nairn. The Culbins cover nearly 4,000 acres, with a weel-marked shore ridge and steep banks rising one hundred feet immediately above sea level. Sloping upwards and inwards from west to east, steadily driven by prevailing westerly winds, they move like slow relentless invaders against the rich farmland of the county of Elgin. Their snail's pace is but one foot a week, or a mile in a century.

But these distant Culbin Sands have not always been either gentle or slow. Hector Boece has a word on them in his Scottish Chronicles where he says that, among the portents that marked the violent death of Malcolm Canmore in 1093, not only did the German Ocean rise against the Northumbrian shore, but 'likewise the land of Moray in Scotland was at the time desolated by the sea, castles subverted from the foundation, some towns destroyed, and the labour of man laid waste, by the discharge of sand from the sea;

monstrous thunders also roaring, horrible and vast.' And at uncertain intervals the uncontrollable sands would take it into their heads to renew their landward invasion in force. Three times have they driven the village of Findhorn from successive sites till now it is safe at last (it hopes) on the right or east shore of the wide Findhorn Bay.

In 1694, the great storm of the late autumn swept the sand inland to engulf the 'big hoose' of the Kinnairds, with a score and more of farms and crofts besides, burying some two hundred people in a grave in which they still lie. The great wind was their gravedigger but the wind would have had nothing to bury them with if the Findhorn had not carried (and still carries in spate) millions of tons of sand from the northern slopes of the Monadh Liath mountains forty miles away. The westward currents of the Moray Firth take the sand from the Findhorn and carry it to the great bar lying off the Culbin coast, the daily tides ferry it to the mainland and, wherever the wind has a mind to it, a consignment is carried up the conveyors in the manner just described.

So were made the famous Culbin Sands that lay their splash of gold across the spreading view from the summit of Cairn Gorm: the same panorama of land and sea that once drew the tribute *Quel ensemble* from my breathless French friend. Today (1947) the climber will not see the Culbin Sands as we saw them, for the Forestry Commission have taken them in hand and now call them the Culbin Forest. If you visit this 'forest' today, you will find that the Commission first put the moving sands into harness by 'fixing' them with a light thatch of brushwood pegged down at short intervals over the whole area and then planted young conifers as permanent binding. Even after several years of this taming, the sands were still unruly and when the British Empire Forestry Conference were taken to see the experiment on July 4th 1947, they saw many young trees buried to a depth of ten feet and more by moving sand. In our day, the golden sands were still uncovered and the wide landscape on which they drew their characteristic line would have held us long once more in that dawn of 1904, were the rest of the day's march not already claiming our attention.

(iii)

This is early morning, and the late afternoon should see us back on Speyside after a circuit of plateau and peak and corrie which will embrace the four main tops, with seven lesser heights as links in the Cairngorm chain. We take our second breakfast at the Marquis Well and design a timetable for the stages: Cairn Lochan, Ben Macdhui, Carn a' Mhaim, the Dee, Beinn Bhrottain, Monadh Mor, Devil's Point, Carn Toul, Sgor an Lochain Uaine, Braeriach, Sron na Lairig, Rothiemurchus.

'I bet we don't do them all,' says Hugh.

'Why not?' says I. 'It's a matter of thirty odd miles and something more than twice the height of Cairn Gorm to climb, so why not, with nearly fifteen hours of daylight and a fine day before us? Though, well … if this little breeze freshens and veers a bit more to the south-east, we may be in mist before we're off Braeriach this afternoon. Anyway, Hugh, my boy, you may remember the saying that failure is the path of least persistence.'

'McGilky's not literate enough to know what that means,' said Hugh. Whereat McGilky laughed his well-known bell-like laugh, saying, 'It's as much fun making the timetable as doing it on our feet.'

A quick reckoning gave two hours and a bit to the top of Ben Macdhui via Cairn Lochan, forty minutes to Carn a' Mhaim, fifteen more down to the Dee, one to two hours up Beinn Bhrottain, half an hour to Monadh Mor, one and a half hours to Carn Toul via the Devil, another half (perhaps more) to the top of Braeriach and two and a half to Rothiemurchus via Sron na Lairig and the Lairig itself; add, say one and a half for loitering, eating and controversy over the things that provoke it. Twelve hours in all, and it's now four o'clock in the morning, so teatime should find us at the Rothiemurchus Triangle once more. Check this by the Peyton–Naismith Rule, and we find we have given ourselves half an hour *under* the allotted time. We shall see.

So, off to Ben Macdhui at 4 am exactly, with the sun now a full hour up the eastern sky and the promise of a fine day as bright as ever. A short spell at a swinging pace takes us past the Black Knuckles for the third time in twelve hours. Leaving the Fiacill Ridge on our right, we skirt the edge of the Corrie of the Snows, where the air is as cold as it ought to be, and reach the fine crag of Cairn Lochan which is seventeen feet short of four thousand. Here are monoliths set in Nature's design of disorder, piled and grooved together to make a wall in tiers of weathered rock and, below them, the great smooth slab framed in a deep snow-wreath. Seen from the seven-mile distance of Aviemore, or from the top of the Slugan Pass, the smooth red bareness of this slab is a marked feature of the wide corrie below Cairn Lochan and figures in most of the descriptions of the difficult rock climbs on the face of the cliff. Below us are the two lochans, the greater shaped like a kidney, which gives its name to the summit on which we stand, and the lesser which got its name from us when we found and christened Allt Eggie*—for this is none other than Lochan a' Cearc, the Hen Tarn.

From Cairn Lochan we make for the Feith Buidhe. The deer are feeding in large numbers in a green hollow by the stream. The young ptarmigan—the 'termagants' of Thomas Kirke's *Modern Account of Scotland* (1679)—rise in low swift flight at our feet, some of them, to be sure, too young to do more than scuttle and fall over themselves among the grey stones. Away to the right, Carn Toul shows his double head now and then above the deep shadow of Lairig, but this is the hour of day for fast walking and we do not wait to gaze around. We are actually on the summit of Ben Macdhui twenty minutes ahead of our own reckoning, but as the distance is a bare four miles and the net rise a matter of eight hundred feet, our allowance was

See Chapter Four

generous. Thus we are at the second stage of the journey by six in the morning, and as we look back across the wide highland that links Cairn Gorm with Ben Macdhui we see once more how much of this range is composed of high broad plateaux—the peneplain left behind after the Ice Age with gouge and chisel and smoothing-plane had sheered and ground away the greater heights that once towered far above the summit on which we now stand.

Here on the heights the season is short. The storms of winter return to their last attack on the wings of March, and April at times brings the heaviest snow of the year. So, the Cairngorm summer comes shy and late, rarely before the middle of May in the mildest seasons, with, perhaps, the first warmth at Whitsun. And the fall of the autumn may follow any moment after the partridge-shooting has begun in the valleys below.

Just before Whitsun, say in an early year, the golden plover and the pipit may be seen on the high stony wastes, the first colours of the flowers begin to glow faintly amid their grey surroundings and, by mid-June, the pale-starred azalea, the moss campion and here and there, though often hard to find, the starry saxifrage which has been called the

London Pride of the Heights. As the summer flowers begin to bloom, the ptarmigan changes his coat, no longer wearing his grey and drab-white disguise but putting on a plumage of black and dark-grey, glossy and groomed, while his hen has a gilded smock under darker wings—white camouflage for eight months, brindled grey-black-gold for the other four. 'Though their colour camouflage is perfect,' says one observer, 'ptarmigan leave a strong ground scent which excites my dogs as keenly as the red grouse or the mountain hare.' But you may walk far and long over the Cairngorms without ever seeing a white hare. Much less plentiful they are than they were a generation ago.

Other companions there are a-plenty: a solan goose over Loch Insh, a pair of herons in Glen Feshie, a crested tit under the Lurcher's Crag. Even above three thousand feet, there are more birds and beasts and flowers in the high hills than the casual climber might suppose: the dunlin, described as a 'bird that frequents European and British shores' but one of our companions on the heights nonetheless; the wheatear, a bird of international touring habits; the snow-bunting, which seems to dislike England but may be found up here or in Turkestan and China; and (with luck) the dainty and rare dotterel, with his striped jockey-cap head and sherry-coloured vest (also a migrant who prefers to follow the rich men of the north to warmer homes in winter); golden eagles above Einich and Loch Avon; and the red deer moving up to the high ground in the late spring.

The High Cairngorms stand like the central keep of a mountain fortress whose outer works are maintained by the whole Grampian system stretching from the estuary of the Tay to Inverness. The Grampian area proper is measured by the thousand in square miles, perhaps seven thousand square miles in all, but the high centre between Spey and Dee covers about four hundred and fifty square miles, the Lairig Pass itself being the diameter across the middle, twenty-seven miles in length from Braemar to Aviemore.

On this central citadel the battlements are broad and the moats are deep. The sharp peaks of other ranges are not its distinguishing feature for, of the four greatest heights, only one (Carn Toul) rises to a sharp point, high apart from the rest. The others are wide ridges, like Braeriach, four thousand feet high, spreading in an almost flat expanse between magnificent corrie walls, or sloping shoulders like Cairn Gorm who has a steep flank only on his eastern side, or gently rising ground of the kind we have traversed this morning, where on the northern slope of Ben Macdhui you can walk for nearly two miles and only rise 790 feet in transit. These level spaces, almost like plains in high land, are a notable feature of the whole Cairngorm system. On Ben A'an and Ben a' Bhuird you can walk seven miles without ever going below 3,500 feet; the Feshie hills, Sgoran Dhu, Sgor Goith, and Carn Ban undulate in gentle lines at something like the same heights, and it has been claimed that a horseman could ride over wide stretches of turf without ever touching a stone. Similarly, you'd be hard put to it to find his true top on Braeriach, if all three tops did not carry cairns to lead you to them, for his summit is as wide an expanse as any in the Monadh Ruadh, and you can spend some hours doing his lofty circuit of cliff and corrie without wasting a moment.

And, as we have already seen this morning, this Cairngorm–Ben Macdhui plateau is an area of something over eight square miles, all of it above the 3,500-foot contour. Grassy in places, holding the never-melted snow in hollows that are the birthplace of streams, covered throughout with the granite debris of the ages which is sometimes spread so smooth that walking is as easy as on the road, the shingly ground clothed here and there with black moss softer under the feet than any lawn, and here and there lying in lines and ridges as if the sand had been swept by a brush or a receding tide had marked the successive moments of its ebb in concentric circles upon the white gravel. Here the embroidery of wind and rain lies spread at the walker's feet, catching his eye till he must stop to admire nature's needlework in which delicate lines weave themselves like the watered silk pattern drawn on the surface of a bowl of liquid by the intense vibration of an aircraft in flight—a design of broken circles and interlacing ripples.

There are two streams to cross on the way up the long slope of Ben Macdhui's northern side, the Greater and the Lesser Rough Water, Garbh Uisge Mor and Beag, both of them on their way to Loch Avon. But there are other springs unknown to the Ordnance Survey, lying like well-set jewels in this wide waste of stone. Here is one of them which has flowed out of the mountainside for no one knows how long, slowly making a little basin for itself, no more than a hand's breadth wide, and deep for its width, watering the roots of a few tiny tufts of growth which nod and tremble in the breeze. It stands out from or, more truly, lies within its stony surroundings like an oasis. A flat boulder spans this miniature well on its upper side, covering the hollowed cup of crystal water, and from under it peep the coloured leaves of cranberry, a finger of wiry moss or a feathery tuft which would be heather if it could. And, at the bottom of the pool, a carpet of silver sand, with here and there a streak of tawny colour which, if shaped aright, might be a 'cairngorm'.

Scores of springs like these crop out of the bare boulder-ridden ground, usually under one of the steeper slopes but sometimes in the middle of the high flat plateaux, and the larger of them make the wells which are marked on the map. I came across one such, the source of the Druie itself, on a hot September afternoon high up on Creag na Chalamain, the Kite's crest, which is one of the north-western outliers of the range, standing partner to Carn Elrig, the Sanctuary, the pair of them like sentinels posted at the mouth of the Lairig. There was no need to obey Joshua's rule of how one drinks in the presence of the enemy and, having no 'coggie' in my pocket, I lay down flat on my face to drink. I became engrossed in the design which the spring had laid out around itself, a little world in miniature, with more colour and variety than one would guess at first glance. It reminded me of nothing so much as the dwarf gardens which the

Japanese make in enamelled bowls, decked out with pygmy trees and shrubs, some of them the actual miniatures of maple and cryptomeria. But one thing no Japanese garden could offer is the pure cold water of the Cairngorms. Theirs is the last word in delicate and sophisticated artifice, mine, one of Nature's careless gifts which you may easily miss if your eyes are not open.

(iv)

But we are not here to star-gaze in crystal pools all day, for there is another high circuit of hills spread before us now. This is Ben Macdhui, and if you climb him today you will find the Cairngorm Club's Indicator, showing on its porcelain disk the panorama of everything visible from this summit, north, south, east and west, on a clear day. There was no such aid to curiosity forty years ago and I am not persuaded that the climber is really better off with it than we were without it. True, the arrow on the porcelain face cannot lie, and is always there to arbitrate the issue whether Morven-in-Helmsdale and Ben Scarab (usually called Scaraben) are separately visible due north of us, and whether the extreme range of vision is one hundred miles or less. Anyway, with no Indicator to guide us this morning, we have no better opportunity from Ben Macdhui than we had three hours ago from Cairn Gorm of settling these issues, or of proving that Largo Law and the Cheviots and the Pentlands and the Lammermuirs are really the southern backcloth of this memorable scene.

On one point there can be no dispute and, as we move south-westerly towards the upper rim of the Corrie of the Tailors' Burn, we pause fascinated before the great picture of Carn Toul, with the Barn Corrie (Coire an t'Sabhail) like a shallow tilted bowl under the ridged summit, and the flowing falling line of his gown from shoulder to heel spreading its lower border over the gathering waters of the Upper Dee. Between Carn Toul and the Sgor an Lochain Uaine, the farthest horizon shows Ben Alder standing above Loch Ericht and, perhaps (but not very sure about this) the nearer and lower top of Ben Udlaman behind Chaoruinn and Am Bhuideanach Beag. Ben Nevis would not show himself, and look as we might in the far gap beyond the Angel's Peak we could not see him.

Soon we have no eyes for the scene around us. The ground falls steeply away at four thousand feet at the brink of the Tailors' Corrie and, though the descent is no Alpine risk, it calls for care of eye and hand and foot. The first stage takes us down the left side of the corrie and, bearing still farther to the left before we are far down the Tailors' Burn (still a steepish drop requiring a careful eye and well-planted feet) we reach the long narrow spur that joins Carn a' Mhaim to Ben Macdhui, Ceann Caol, the Headland of the Strait and Narrow Way. We pause to note two things. First, that the *col* of the language of the Alps is related to the *caol* of the Gaelic, which is both an adjective meaning narrow and a noun meaning a strait, a firth or narrows—a reminder that both French and Gaelic have many roots in common going down to Latin and Greek: *fhir, vir; eaglais, ecclesia, eglise; diabhol, diabolus, diable, devil; sgoilear, scholar, ecolier; muir, mare, mer,* and so on.

The second point that comes to mind is the tale that gives that flat, ribbed stone below us its name, Clach an Tailleur, the Tailors' Stone. Tailors have a knack of breeding fables about themselves and the Three Tailors of Badenoch who are the name-fathers of this great stone have some of the same flavour about them as Canning's Three Tailors of Tooley Street who, in their Humble Address to the House of Commons, claimed to be 'We, the People of England'. Our three Speyside Tailors wagered that, on the last day of the year, they would dance the reel three times in the three dells before midnight, on the Dell of Abernethy, the Dell of Rothiemurchus and the Dell of Mar, and see the New Year in on Deeside. This Hogmanay bet cost them their lives. They saw the New Year in indeed, but lying side by side frozen stiff in the Lairig snow on the spot where their Stone stands below us in the narrowing mouth of the pass, on the lower slope of Carn a' Mhaim.

By the same token, others have paid the same price as these tailors for challenging the Cairngorms unwarily in winter. Late in December 1927, two Glasgow men, Hugh Barrie and Thomas Baird, set out from a cottage near Tullochgrue in Upper Rothiemurchus to walk through the pass, having said that they would sleep at the Corrour Bothy under Carn Toul and return to Rothiemurchus across Carn Toul and Braeriach. By New Year's Day no word of them had reached Rothiemurchus but on January 2nd Baird was found, two miles below Loch Einich near the first bothy. He was still alive, but unconscious, and died in the arms of his rescuers before he could tell his story. Deep snow covered Glen Einich and it was not till the spring that Barrie's body was found two miles up the glen near the loch itself. Barrie's grave stands below the northern mouth of the Lairig Ghru near the spot whence he and Baird set out on their fatal walk. The cairn over the grave is crowned with a large stone recording the death of both men, with the words below, 'Find me a wind-swept boulder for a bier'. Five years later, again on New Year's Day, two lives were lost in the same way. A cairn on the right bank of the Allt a Coire Cas on Cairn Gorm marks the spot where Alistair Mackenzie and Duncan Ferrier of Grantown-on-Spey were found dead, seven days after they had left Loch Morlich on their way to the Shelter Stone of Loch Avon. The Scottish Mountaineering Club record these accidents in order to 'enforce the warnings already given for caution in expeditions in these lofty and remote mountains'.

At the edge of the broader northern end of Ceann Caol, we look over the rim of a little corrie in which the burn called Allt Carn a' Mhaim rises, and then pass on to the narrowing shoulder of the col on our way to the far end of Carn a' Mhaim. Ceann Caol draws little attention to itself as a rule, being no more than the coupling that links a lesser to a greater hill, but it has nonetheless one claim to be unique, for there is no other ridge of quite the same kind anywhere in the High Cairngorms. From the left bank of the Tailors' Burn, over a stretch of some eight hundred yards, it grows steadily narrower and, though never shaved to a true knife-edge, it deserves the description given to it by the Scottish Mountaineering Club: 'exhilarating'.

Two miles from the Tailors' Burn, we reach Carn a' Mhaim herself and here the panorama calls the walker to halt and look. On the left, the Carn a' Mhaim Burn runs down to join the Luibeg, and in front the valley of the Dee stretches for miles in the foreground of a fine skyline of Perthshire hills, with Aberdeen's Lochnagar tracing its crest on the eastern horizon. On the right Beinn Bhrottain rises steeply above Glen Guisachan, the Devil's Point thrusts his cleaving edge above Corrie Odhar and the twin eaves of Carn Toul—'the incomparable pair of brethen'—lift once more their unique profile against the blue morning sky. Beyond, the down-sweeping outline of Carn Toul, the deep amphitheatre of Corrie Brochain and the Rugged Corrie—more guessed than actually seen—serves to throw up in sharp perspective the eastern end of the great ridge of Braeriach. Carn a' Mhaim is thus not only herself a jewel, but an outlook tower surveying one of the great scenes of the Cairngorms.

And now, down to the bank of the Dee, where the red slabs of granite lie in the bed of the stream and the Fir Tree Burn comes out of Glen Guisachan to join its partner. Whatever my two partners may do, I am going to sit on that tuft on the bank of the stream and soap the outer side of the thin pair of socks under the heavy brown Harris stockings. It is best to do it at the beginning of the day but the Shelter Stone was a cold dressing-room this morning and I've lost nothing by putting it off to this sunny moment on the Upper Dee. An old-fashioned trick, you say! No doubt, but it will carry a pair of feet in comfort through the longest day and prolong the life of stockings and socks alike. Don't be put off by any mildly patronising contempt for sole-soapers like me. In this, as in some other matters, *experto crede*. There are old fashions that will long outlive new fangles, and this is one of them.

Hugh watched the process of a moment, with his eyes glinting over the bowl of his pipe, and when he had his shag drawing well, he said, 'May I have the loan of your soap when you've done? These boots of mine are a bit heavy.'

'They look heavy to me,' said I, handing over the slice of kitchen soap. 'I learned my first lesson in boots from Peyton, and my second from the old fitter in Allan's. You know the old chap: sits back on his heels, with his spectacles near the end of his nose and his hands under his apron, and says, "Wull that dae noo?" He said about climbing boots, "Ye have tae balance the wecht and the welts and the nails. Ye dinna need anything braid i' the way o' welts and gin' yer nails are the richt kin' o' saft iron they'll hold a'thing. And the wecht needna be more'n about three an a half pun'. A wide welt is jest a danger tae ye when ye're on the Bad Step between Scavaig and Loch Coruisk. And when ye get there ye'll mind what Ah'm tellin' ye."'

'Well,' said Hugh, 'mine are wide enough, in all conscience...'

'And I bet yours are a good pound heavier than mine,' I said, 'and that'll mean that you have to lift something like twenty tons more than I do, during a long day like this.'

'Rot!'

'It isn't rot. You admit that each of your feet is lifting half a pound more than mine at each step, and on a day like this we shall cover thirty-five miles and climb close on nine thousand feet. Now,' said I, quoting authority, 'old Peyton used to say that you take at least three thousand steps to the mile when climbing a mountain, which gives us a little sum to do:

$$\frac{105,000}{2} = 52,500 \text{ lbs} = 23.4 \text{ tons} \qquad QED.\text{'}$$

Hugh blew a cloud of fragrant smoke up towards the snout of the Devil. 'Gosh,' said he, 'it sounds incredible, but I suppose you're right.'

'Right?' quoth I. 'It's proved by Bill Peyton and Allan's old fitter, not to mention all the professors of Natural Philosophy since Archimedes. And just to finish the old chap's sermon on shoe-leather: "Ye munna lat the 'boots' at the hotel pit them at the fire tae dry: it fair kills the leather, and ye'll no be shinnin' them wi' blackin' forbye. Naethin's but guid honest grease for them, Ah'm tellin' ye."'

This junction of the Dee and the Guisachan Burn is our crossroads. If we were faint-hearted or late, we should ignore Beinn Bhrottain and the Monadh Mor and make our steep way straight for the Devil's Point. But we are neither late nor faint-hearted (we have indeed gained over half an hour on our timetable) so we can attack Beinn Bhrottain from his eastern side, thus avoiding the awkward slabs that make his north *glacis* a difficult climb for which we have little time to spare today.

In this idle sunny moment by the Dee, as we look at the red plates of rock in the bed of the stream, we are tempted to call a longer halt than the timetable allows.

'We'll let Hugh finish that pipe,' says I, 'and then we must go on.' Party spirit takes hold as we bandy words over the pros of the Guisachan route and the cons of the eastern approach by the stream that we had once christened 'Robbie Burns'—its Gaelic name being Caochan Roibidh, which is said to be a corruption of *roibhe* or bearded.

'Obviously,' says McGilky, 'it's shorter by the glen.'

'Mebbe, though I wouldn't bet on it,' say I, 'and it's a darned sight wetter anyway, in parts. There's a lot of bog in Glen Guisachan and even if we didn't get stuck, we might get caught on those nasty slabs round the corner on the north face which aren't easy work. I plump for the climb along the steep straight side facing the Dee.'

And so on, till Hugh knocks the ashes out of his pipe, which is the signal to depart, while McGilky is heard murmuring something that sounds like a pidgin

Latin version of *Eeny Meeny Miney Mo* to decide the route we shall take.

'That settles it: the glen for me,' says McGilky.

Hugh seemed to care little which choice was made. He murmured one of his favourite passages from *Alice* in which Tweedledee might be said to be tweedling Hamlet's famous words in the Fifth Act: '"Contrariwise," continued Tweedledee, "if it was so, it might be; and if it were so, it would be; but as it isn't, it ain't. That's logic." And I think,' concluded Hugh, 'that your mountain logic is better than McGilky's.'

So McGilky took the high road by Glen Guisachan alone and we the low road parallel to the Dee on the east flank of Beinn Bhrottain, with the inevitable bet which was the shorter and who would first reach the top of Beinn Bhrottain. My own guess, in spite of what I had just said, gave McGilky the advantage of about half a mile and somewhat easier going, provided—and it was a proviso with plenty of chances in it—he avoided the overlapping slabs that are worse than they look. So we parted. Hugh and I crossed the Dee and the Guisachan just above their junction and struck down the valley in a line upwards and aslant the steep slope of Beinn Bhrottain's eastern wall. The cliff above is no corrie but a straight craggy fringe, and the course we took led just below the point where scree and boulder give place to precipices of varying height and pitch. It was rough and stiff going till we reached Robbie Burns himself and, by his aid, proved once more the old truth that a burn is a good guide, going up or down, except where he breaks into waterfall and then you must leave him. The steepest part of the climb we found in the two hundred feet below the 2,500-foot contour and we left him there, bearing to the right with the rivalry of our invisible partner to spur us on. Forty minutes of determined climbing brought us to the edge of the flat eastern top, where the figure of McGilky sauntering towards the main cairn five hundred yards away showed us that he had circumvented the slabs and that we had lost our bet.

The cairn itself is unique. It is encircled by a drystone dyke which, though somewhat broken-down, shows that someone had reason to build more than the usual hilltop cairn. Otherwise the summit of Beinn Bhrottain calls for no remark. The Scottish Mountaineering Club call it 'featureless'. It might be any one of a dozen flattish tops set so far back from corrie or crag that, in itself, it has little distinction. But as the platform of an outlook tower, it almost deserves an Indicator of its own. Doubtless it has never had one because it is a comparatively neglected hill, but as we slowly survey the circle of the view, we resolve to give it a high place among the 'crows' nests' of the Cairngorms. We sit on the broken dyke to look across Glen Guisachan at the perspective of the Devil and Carn Toul, with a hint of the Angel behind, turn a little to see whether Carn a' Mhaim puts her best foot forward in this direction, though the lower edge of her skirt is hidden by the cliffs above the Dee, or, a little further round, see the tops of Beinn a' Bhuird and Ben A'an ranged *en echelon*, crowded together, and so on round the horizon, with the longest view stretched far down the valley of the Dee to the crest of Lochnagar away to the left, peeping out behind Carn Cloich-mhuilinn.

In the dip between the top of Beinn Bhrottain and his neighbour Monadh Mor, the rim of the Battle Corrie gives a closer view of Glen Guisachan, and across it to the right you may see how the Devil's Point loses much of his point when seen from behind, in spite of the collar of craggy rock that surrounds his Bod. And as we look down to Glen Guisachan itself, an almost level green valley stretching for two miles to the Dee, we speculate on its appearance when it first got its name, the Fir Tree Glen. Was it so noted for its firs that they gave it their own name? Or was there some conifer, hardier than his fellows, who held out in the glen long after they had fallen before the storm? The bed of the valley is actually on the edge of the normal Cairngorm tree line, which runs true at about 1,700 feet. But did the tree line always lie on that contour? Or were the trees found higher up in former times? Or, if not higher up, at least *farther ben in the hills*? If local story goes for anything, the broken sluice at the lower end of Glen Einich, far over there below Braeriach's Einich Cairn, was built to provide a flood on which to float tree trunks down the Bennie Burn to Rothiemurchus. There is no doubt that the tale runs that way but I have always been a sceptic about it, for why carry 'coals to Newcastle' in the shape of logs from Loch Einich, when the Forest of Rothiemurchus was full of them?

By the same token, the sluice on the Luineag at Loch Morlich has the same origin in local story, but only provokes the same query. And it was not till many years later that my rhetorical question was silenced by my old friend the Revd A E Robertson of the Scottish Mountaineering Club, who pointed out to me that the logs were not floated down from

Einich, but that it was necessary to dam the loch in order to make a head of water sufficient to provide a strong freshet which could lift the great trunks felled in Rothiemurchus Forest much lower down. This was an artificial 'spate' to float the logs down the lower Druie to the Spey, which carried them to the little shipyards of Kingston and Port Gordon on the Moray Firth. Those who remember Elizabeth Grant's *Memoirs of a Highland Lady* will recall her characteristic account of the 'log-floating' of 1810.

The peaty bottom of Glen Guisachan itself answers the question about its name but I had never seen the evidence till a later date than 1904 and so our speculation of that summer could flourish, as it will in that best of all conditions for speculative luxuriance, the absence of evidence. On both sides of the burn, but more freely on its left bank, which gets more sunshine than the right, throughout its whole length right up to a point where the banks begin to close steeply upon it at about 1,800 feet, the stumps and roots of trees are to be found embedded in the dark soil in considerable numbers. They show that in days gone by, Glen Guisachan *was* the glen of the fir trees, though today only a birch or two still holds out. But, to be sure, the birch has a way of climbing higher than the others; and it plants itself out most pertinaciously. The stumps of many an ancient forest must lie concealed beneath the deep cover of the peat. Here the peat in its turn has decayed and the gaunt ghosts of dead trees come up to the light of day once more.

This Battle Corrie from which we look into Glen Guisachan is as good a study of its kind as any of the more famous corries on Braeriach or Lochnagar. It may not claim to rival Braeriach's Garbh Choire or the colossal pit of the Black Spout under Cac Carn Beag, but it has a quality that puts it among its greatest neighbours and the very fact that the rockfalls below its two southern promontories never see the sun gives it great boldness in light and shadow. It is gouged in irregular depth out of the western shoulder of Beinn Bhrottain and if the cheese-scoop of the Ice Age had only cut a little deeper into the col behind it, there would have been another dark little lairig between Beinn Bhrottain and the lower top of Monadh Mor—to which we climb in a matter of ten minutes, turning our backs with regret on the Battle Corrie. But on the upward way, a few minutes west from the corrie's edge, there is one point, easily missed and perchance no one else has ever sought out, where you may compare two queens, Carn a' Mhaim to the north-east and Sron na Banrigh to the south-west in Glen Feshie. These two are cast in the same mould. Little of either of them is visible and that little only for a moment from the chosen stance on the Aberdeen–Inverness border between the two tops of Monadh Mor, but there is just enough of them to be seen to recall remembrance of their pleasant lines. So here we pause to look fore and aft at the Carn and the Sron.

From this broad plateau of Monadh Mor, we can see again that these Cairngorms are in very truth 'highlands', steeply raised from the surrounding lowland on the eastern side and sloping more smoothly downwards to the west and the north. Monadh Mor is the southern containing-wall of the wide quadrangle of peat and moss and running water that bears the name of the Great Moss, An Moine Mor, and spreads its greatest length for four miles between the head of Glen Fhearnagan and the summit of Carn Toul. Even at its narrowest, it is never less than a mile wide but broadens again down the comparatively gentle gradient of the course of the Luineag, the Sguirnach and the Eidart, which drain the basin of An Moine Mor into Glen Feshie. Below us is the Nameless

Knoll, An Cnap Gun Ainm, which owes to us the only name it has ever had. We composed the name on a later outing in one of those disputatious digressions on place-names in the hills which eat up time but give a remembered flavour to the spot when they take place. On that occasion, we recalled the half-hearted attempt already made in the 'Munro' tables to christen our Cnap as the 'Bump-of-the-Lochan-of-the-Bump'. This, we judged, was an adequate and tautological way of making a cat chase its own tail. Hence our new title for him—'The-Little-Hill-Without-a-Name'—which will, we hope, find its way into the currency of the Ordnance Survey. To the right is Loch nan Stuirteag whose earlier name—Suarach (miserable)—still stands on the older maps.

(v)

We descend from Monadh Mor to the loch, passing it on our left hand and looking down Glen Guisachan to note that no less than twelve streams feed the main burn which runs out of the loch itself. And, turning to look over our right shoulder, as we pass beyond the loch, we catch a memorable glimpse of the Battle Corrie once more.

By this time we have almost doubled back on our tracks round the hairpin bend of the head of Glen Guisachan. Our course takes us along the top of the craggy northern wall of the glen, just below three thousand feet, whence we strike up the back of the Devil's Point to arrive on the top of his projecting bow and gaze down on the Dee and the rising line of the Lairig Ghru, with the mass of Ben Macdhui on the left, and immediately opposite, the pleasing lines of Carn a' Mhaim.

The Devil's Point is polite English for the naked and expressive Gaelic, Bod am Diabhol, or Deamhain. He is what he is because the process of denudation and the earth movement of earlier times excavated Corrie Odhar on one side, ploughed the deep hollow of Glen Guisachan on the other and raised his own sharp plough-shape with a striking individual note between them. And how different he can look, not only on different days and in different weather, but from one side or the other. From Deeside, below Carn a' Mhaim, he is a cone, with fine sweeping flanks, not perhaps as distinctive a cone, nor standing so well out on all sides from his surroundings as Carn Elrig at the other end of the Lairig, but a striking conical hill nonetheless. Or look at him from behind, and you will probably not expect to find him finish in a cairn at the cliff's edge like some of his greater neighbours. These are not his finest foot-forward, nor his most characteristic face. You must see him from the edge of his own western corrie, or from a station near the Lairig's watershed, or from the extreme eastern slope of Braeriach, and then you will see why his head has been called the bow of a battleship.

As we pass round the edge of the Soldier's Corrie, a built-up patch of the upper corrie wall catches the eye. And whether you gauge it with the naked eye or with the field-glasses, you will swear your oath that it is a 'retainer' placed there by the hand of man to hold the rockface in position lest it fall away. Nonetheless, this is Nature's work, not 'stone graven by art or man's device'. Nor is it the most remarkable of its kind in the Cairngorms for, as the Scottish Mountaineering Club's guide has it, the granite of these hills is often 'weathered into horizontal slabs, so well defined and so regular as to give the impression of titanic masonry'. All over the High Cairngorms, the Master Mason has left enduring traces of his work and sometimes you can almost believe that Stonehenge itself has been erected to crown a corrie wall or to set up an elemental temple of worship to the Spirit of the Hills.

If you go over to Glen Einich and climb to the point where the striking gullies of Sgoran Dubh rise out of the detritus and scree of the lower slope, looking up you will see the rock seamed in lines so regular, with the rectangular edges of dressed builder's blocks, that whole stretches of the face look like a massive wall of hewn stone. And in the uppermost tiers of Cairn Lochan, the grand western rampart of Cairn Gorm, there is more of the same masonic work. The Shelter Stone Crag itself, seen from the lower northern side of Loch A'an, has the regular rounded form of a great keep. Those Knuckles and Tors of Cairn Gorm and the Barns of Beinn Mheadhoin look as if they were waiting their completion by the titanic chisel, or maybe they are leftovers of the Great Builder's Yard. They have not always found favour, for George Fennell Robson, the artist of 1814, described the Grampian summit as 'often disfigured by rocky slabs like those of Ben Avon'. You will doubtless reject the Robsonian criterion and if you would see how the Earth can build herself a wall of really great stones, you must go to the top of Cac Carn Beag, walk to the edge of the famous Black Spout and there you will see a stronger battlement than ever man built, crowning the cliffs of Lochnagar.

Ben Macdhui and Loch A'an

The top of Carn Toul is not built thus. Nature, in shaping his head like a House of the Twin Gables, took care that he demand the greatest effort from his conquerors in their last moments before they reach the summit. Here is no orderly array of great stones laid in symmetry together but a disorderly rabble, heaped together and sprawling apart with intent to twist the ankle of the incautious. And, in proud distinction from his fellows in the range, he presents no spreading carpet of smooth gravel and rounded shoulder but a unique top sheered steeply away in all directions. But we are in danger of provoking confident protests from Braeriach, from Lochnagar, even from Lurcher's Crag. This bragging of Carn Toul will never do, even if it is vicarious. It provokes Braeriach in a deep bass murmur to tout the claim of his neighbour with the name of Garbh Choire, while Lochnagar calls from his distant throne to remind Carn Toul that he has a whole crescent of gullies and corries, in which the Black Spout alone can swallow all that the arrogant Barn Hill—spoken in what accents of contempt—can offer.

But at the end of the account, and granting the full force of the pleas of his great partners, Carn Toul takes pride of place. If it is true of the whole Cairngorm range—and it is certainly true that you must see it from all angles, at all seasons, in all weathers, by day and by night, returning again and again—it is doubly true of Carn Toul.

There are many points of vantage from which to see him, but three of these show him at his best. Yet all three are quite different and no two judges will agree which is the great 'best'. Nor is it possible to put them on the same footing, for in none of the three can we compare like with like. That view (we saw it a little way back) from somewhere below the four thousand-foot contour of Ben Macdhui, bearing south-west from the summit, leaves you breathless. If you stand at the right point and on the right day, there seems to be nothing but dark and deep space between you and Carn Toul's sharp ridged head, and you can see why he was christened the Hill of the Two Gables. 'Barn' is the usual English form of his Gaelic name Carn an t'Sabhail, and it sounds well enough as we heard it a moment ago in Lochnagar's sharp sneer, but it is a poor word to convey what you will see. The characteristic feature of Carn Toul is the steep roof-like appearance of the line which joins his two tops. In this feature, he stands alone. Whether you see it first in the long four-mile perspective across An Moine Mor from the west, or in the more formidable nearer view from Ben Macdhui, his unique silhouette prints an unforgettable picture on the memory.

The most strongly contrasted picture breaks on the view of the walker coming up Glen Dee. When the Devil's Point is well out of the way on the left and you are approaching the Corrour Bothy, perhaps a little way up the western flank of Carn a' Mhaim, you see Carn Toul as you can never see any of the others. He stands out by himself, solid and broad-based, poised apart from his great neighbours, except for the impertinent nose of the Devil's Point. The mountain's eastern flank sweeps from a single peak (the double summit is not visible from here) down to the bed of the Dee in an unbroken curve of two thousand feet, with a massive dignity and a rich dark splendour all his own. Or you may see something of the same view, the other way round, from a point much higher up the Pass, whence Carn Toul seems to wear a russet mantle stretching in graceful line from that buckle on his shoulder between the Barn Corrie and Coire Lochain Uaine down to the bottom of the valley, where the winding course of the Dee embroiders a fringe of silver on the trailing border of his cloak.

The third coign of vantage is far on the other side of the range. We glanced at it a moment ago, the long view across An Moine Mor of the double-headed penthouse of Carn Toul, but time forbids us today to go over to Carn Ban four miles away in order to see how the unique roof of the 'Barn Hill' points its sign manual on the skyline.

So we move to our next port of call, threading our way with caution over and down the great obstructing boulders of Carn Toul's summit, round the serrated rim above the Green Loch, on a dizzy edge at times, till we come up the narrowing ridge which reaches its apex in Sgor an Lochain Uaine. If, on occasion, one may lapse into its popular, but wrong, English name, the 'Angel's Peak', it is just as well to remember that this misnomer has no warrant but the remark, attributed to Alexander Copland of Aberdeen, that 'the balance must be kept round the Eaves of the Barn, and if there be a Devil on one side, the Devil must not have it all his own way and there should be an Angel on the other.' Good enough to warrant, no doubt, and many a Cairngorm name has been given for more trivial reasons, if indeed an eggshell* be a triviality. But this light-hearted anglicising of the Gaelic is false to the original and misses the pertinence of names which nearly always express something appropriate to the scene. Copland himself may send the posthumous retort that 'Green Loch Peak, which is the correct translation of Sgor an Lochain Uaine, is both poor and repetitive', for there are many 'Green Lochs' and many 'Sgors' in the Cairngorms. In this respect, Copland's 'sobriquet' has a kind of left-handed point and, since it has won colloquial currency, we may admit that the Angel's Peak has come to stay.

And pity 'tis that we cannot stay long on this promontory above the highly-perched Green Loch. It may not have all the panoramic quality of the

*See Chapter Four and Appendix Two.

Devil, for Carn Toul blocks part of the eastern view, but it is so good a stance for the survey of the grand amphitheatre of the Rough Corrie (Garbh Choire Mor), with the Braeriach cairn in the topmost gallery seat, and there is so much to catch the eye in and around the corrie itself, that one might stay long and never exhaust the attractive interest of the scene. This Sgor is more nearly a true peak than the Devil's Point itself, besides being eight hundred feet higher. It thrusts its nose upward, while the Devil seems to advance forwards. Its crescent-scarp and skyward tilt give the climber the sense of being raised on a ledge apart from his surroundings. Northwards, it looks straight into the narrowing gut of the pass between Sron na Lairig and the March Burn, and towards it from the broken crest of Creag an Leth-choin runs the craggy fringe of the steep eastern Lairig wall, like 'the frieze of that colossal temple raised to Time'.

Below it, to the right, Lochan Uaine seems too dark to be green but at its shallow edge it begins to justify its name, while here and there on its surface the reflection of green patches in the surrounding corrie spreads an olive tinge on the smooth water, like a sombre silk coverlet shot with an overtone, as of seaweed at low tide. No one has suggested that the water of this Lochan Uaine is green because the fairies wash their clothes in it, for that pleasant legend belongs by right to the Green Loch of the Ryvoan Pass. Nor do the records of Daoine Sith corroborate the poet's statement—it is James Hogg that speaks—that he had an encounter with one of these fairy laundresses who had hair like green seaweed and eyes 'like the boiled e'en o' a cod's head'.

Lochan Uaine sends the first of many tributaries to join the Dee, and if the cascade that pours over the outer rim of the corrie bowl below us were only a little bigger, Lochan Uaine and not Braeriach would be the true source of the river and that little stream would be the Dee, instead of being only Allt Lochan Uaine, and losing even the name after a few hundred feet of fall. But even when the rainstorm has filled the lochan and made it brim over in a foaming waterfall, it cannot change names with the Dee which rises far over on our left on the high ground of the Braeriach ridge. The Dee claims to run faster and to fall proportionately farther in its short run to the sea than any other Scottish river and it boasts that, between Garbh Choire Dhe (the Dee's Rough Corrie) and Aberdeen, there is no loch to arrest even for a moment its rapid flow. Garbh Coire Dhe is the minor chamber of the

Great Rough Corrie itself and its deep cavity is one of the features which entitle the parent corrie to call itself great. We shall pass round the wide rim of the main corrie in a moment but before we leave Sgor an Lochain Uaine we may take our bearings and measure this amphitheatre by space and time.

The gulf is 1,500 feet deep and, as the crow flies, the distance from our Sgor to the main top of Braeriach is about a mile, but to reach it round the deep corries, the Rough One and the Dee, one has between two and three miles to walk: a full three miles if we visit all three tops on the way. Before we set out, we can see with a slight effort of imagination why this Brindled Brae takes his shape as a great crescent held up by walls of rock. On the north and west, the wall is deeply curved in four great corries and a lesser groove: Coire Dhondail, Coire Lochan, Coire Ruadh and Coire Beanidh, with Coire Bogha Cloich between the first two. On the east and south, still greater corries form the great moat that separates Braeriach from Carn Toul: the Great Rough Corrie, the Corrie of the Dee and, the finest of all, the Porridge Cauldron (Coire Brochain) whose walls fall sheer from the main cairn itself. I doubt whether there is another spot in the whole range where the high tops enclose a more grandiose circuit of buttress, rock-bowl and cliff. Nor are there many summits that reveal better than Sgor an Lochain Uaine how these hills were made.

No one can appreciate Braeriach, the second highest mountain in the Cairngorms, merely by looking for his highest point, or by climbing to reach it. For not only are there three summits within about one hundred feet of one another in height, but they are separated by something over a mile of wide, big, bare space held high at four thousand feet by the walls which we can see from the Angel's Peak. 'A mere ascent to the highest point,' says Sir Henry Alexander of the Scottish Mountaineering Club, 'is not enough to give us adequate idea of Braeriach. The mountain is one to be wandered over, and, when so explored on a long summer's day or taken in sections on different excursions, it becomes strangely interesting and impressive.'

Today, we have not a long summer's day before us. We have already spent nearly twelve hours on our mountain circuit since dawn and we must move on, descending 350 feet to the edge of the inner recess of the Great Rough Corrie and round its neighbour, the Rough Corrie of the Dee. Back from the edge of the

Dee Corrie is the source of the river itself, marked by a small white cairn standing on a bank of moss. Here the Dee comes forth, not like a gentle spring but a full-fledged stream, gushing out of the ground and flowing fast to the edge of the corrie where it pours in white foam over the rim in a broken cascade, now tumbling among the rocky slabs, now leaping in sheer waterfall till it reaches the heavy scree five hundred feet below, where it is soon joined by the burn from the Rough Corrie itself and, a little later, by the stream which we saw overflowing from Lochan Uaine a short while ago.

The last stage of this Cairngorm circuit was quickly made. Leaving the Porridge Cauldron summit of Braeriach—and how unwillingly will any climber leave the great platform—we struck north across the broad breast of Braeriach to the high crest of Corrie Ruadh till we came to the spur between this corrie and its eastern neighbour, Corrie Beanidh. Here the scene opens out into a spreading landscape with distance and wide perspectives leading to the northern horizon of the hills beyond Aviemore. It has not the finished grace of Cairn Gorm's panorama, for it lacks the green-gold foreground of Glen More, but as a more monochrome variant of the same scene, it has points of its own. Beneath our feet is the contrast of two corries, Ruadh the more precipitous, Beanidh less sharp, with its rock edges worn away and softened with grass. As we paused on the rim between them, a picture greater than either came into my mind. I looked at my watch.

'Are you game,' said I, 'to see the best sight of all? It'll add another hour to the day's work, but it's only a bit past two and even with the new detour we should be home by six.'

'I'm game,' said Hugh.

'What's the game?' said McGilky.

'You'll see.'

We set off westwards along the crest of Corrie Ruadh till we came in sight of the highest of all the corrie lochs in the Cairngorms, Loch Coire an Lochain. We scrambled down the steep west flank of Corrie Lochan till we came to the bed of snow which lies late in summer to make the foreground of Braeriach's finest profile. Many Corrie Lochans there are in the Cairngorms, but none that excel this tarn under the north face of the mountain.

After a pause, Hugh said, 'Which way now?'

'Bear left,' I said, 'for Einich, or right for the Lairig.'

'Toss,' said McGilky, and the coin sent us back to the Lairig. Turning east again, we crossed the mouths of Braeriach's three great northern corries and, holding a level course round the shoulder of Sron na Lairig, we reached the line of crags which face Creag an Leth-choin across the pass. Skirting their crinkled edge, we decided not to take the rough way by Carn Elrig and came down into the lovely woods of the upper Forest of Rothiemurchus in the late afternoon.

On the way down Hugh stopped to tie a loose lace and then spread the map on his knees. We could see him scratching his head over some puzzle. When he overtook us, he said, 'I thought you called that corrie to our left up there *Goundle*, or something of the sort. I can't find it: the only one on the map is *Dondle*.' So he pronounced it.

'That's it all right, but *DH* is *G* in the Gaelic and the name of the Corrie—Goundle or Gownt'll—is the Dale of the Stirks. Elizabeth Grant, a hundred years ago, anglicised it as Gowanthill, but then she called Sgor Gaoith *Scarigons*.'

'Cattle as far up as that? The name seems a bit off its proper beat.'

'Not really. Cattle were grazed in the old days far higher up than they are now.'

The truth is that there are many high corries and glens in the Cairngorms which bear witness to the herding of cattle, perhaps also of goats, in remote corners of the hills. There are scores of names, of which Dhondail is only one, which are derived from these high grazings, and one of the earlier Grants owed his unusual name, John Corrour, to his birthplace in one of them. He was born under the cliffs of Coire Odhar, which is Corrour, when his mother was up at the south end of Glen Einich during the summer grazing, and if you look down from the top of the cliffs you will see a wide patch of green grass to this day, which formerly was the scene of an annual migration from Rothiemurchus. To perpetuate the memory of his unusual birthplace, John Corrour left money in his will to build a shieling under Corrie Odhar 'where there shall always be meal in it'.

Back at the Dell of Rothiemurchus and sitting on the lawn looking up to the mountains in which we had spent the past twenty-three hours, we made our reckoning. From one o'clock in the morning (to be precise it was 1.05 am when we crossed the Garbh Uisge near the head of Loch A'an) we had covered thirty-eight miles and climbed 9,300 feet. And if the whole round from Loch Morlich be reckoned, we had spent twenty-three hours in covering forty-five miles and climbing something over 12,000 feet, the excess of three hours [compared to Naismith's Rule] being almost exactly the time spent at the Shelter Stone. The Naismith Rule usually works out truly on the average for any outing of normal scope and ours was perhaps just a trifle outside the ordinary rule. But, rule or no rule, 'Gentlemen in England now abed' might well envy us our day.

Four
The Lairig Ghru

And now I cross the span of the years, to look at the same scene with older eyes. Two wars and much tree-felling have changed the Rothiemurchus landscape in many places. In 1943 the 'Public Footpath to Braemar' lost itself in a maze of tents and mule lines on the banks of the Druie near Coylum Bridge and many million feet of timber were carried away to feed the war. At Ault Dhru itself, the Sappers left their mark behind them: no less than three bridges over the stream, built as 'exercises for troops in river-crossing', where there was only the Cairngorm Club's iron footbridge of 1912 before, and the sight of one of these, a solid well-tied structure of trunks, provoked one to wonder whether it might be the ominous forerunner of a road through the Lairig, horrid shadow of a coming event. We must live in the hope that no such vandal folly will be perpetrated and that the project of a Feshie–Dee road will be likewise rejected. What Wade spared, let no man deface.

Fortunately, none of the war changes cut more than skin deep. The walk up the Lairig is as it ever was, though perhaps rougher than it must have been when cattle were driven through the Pass from west to east in former days. And there are few hill walks to beat it, just as there is no pass in the British Isles that can rival the Lairig.

So we enter it once more, not on ambitious mountain-conquest bent but led by the Feng Shui of the Pass to follow where the finger of whim or chance may point. The northern threshold of the Lairig is laid on the rising ground of the last outskirt of the Forest of Rothiemurchus and through it the path leads by the ruined cottages of the former hamlet of Ault Dhru, where the level greensward suggests a pasture of bygone times where crofters kept their few cattle. But, in fact, there were more than crofters here two hundred years ago. We find the best evidence in Elizabeth Grant's *Memoirs of a Highland Lady,* where she tells many stories of her clan but none more vivid than those that made Macalpine a legend in the countryside. Macalpine was Fourth Laird of Rothiemurchus, son of Laird James and Grizzel Mor—the same Grizzel who held the island castle of Loch an Eilean against the partisans of James II (and VII) in

1688. He built The Doune in 1710, or thereabouts, and the tales of him, says Elizabeth, are still to be heard by those who bring an ear for the Gaelic. The word 'still' is of date early in the eighteen hundreds.

Half an hour's walk brings us to the edge of the tree line, where the path runs along a ridged bank high above the stream, and the first foreground ahead of us is marked in the straight lines of the moraine left behind by the glacier after the last of the ice had melted and these hills were changed from high alps to the massive tableland which we now know as the Cairngorms. On either side of the Pass, just above the moraine banks, there are two sentinel outposts, Carn Elrig on the right, the Castle Hill, and Creag na Chalamain on the left, while straight ahead the Lurcher's Crag with its black edge of rock dominates the first part of the long defile. We turn off the path below the Big Stone, follow the course of the burn that

The Lairig Ghru

comes off Creag na Chalamain and after pausing to look into the spring, turn sharp to the right to climb the first top of the Lurcher's Crag. This is another of those tablelands which lie on the Cairngorm heights and though it is one of the lesser plateaux, it is a good mile long, with the spike of the Crag about half-way.

Over this crag in days gone by, a deerhound leapt to his death in hot pursuit of his quarry which, by one account, was a fox raised over on Cairn Gorm and, by another, a deer which had been hunted all the way from the Ryvoan Pass beyond Loch Morlich. The Cairn Gorm, or fox, version of the story probably accounts for the insistence by some local legend-peddlers that this name of the Hound's Cliff truly belongs to the Fiacill Ridge which separates Coire Cas and the Snowy Corrie on the north-western wall of Cairn Gorm himself. That there was a sturdy mongrel hound and that he came to grief over a crag, no one doubts; nor can anyone doubt that his name has clung so long to the crags over the Lairig that it cannot now be taken away. In any event, we are now on Creag an Leth-choin and find it a good excuse for a pause both for breath and for sightseeing.

The spike of this craggy ridge commands the pass from Rothiemurchus to the watershed near the March

Burn, with a spreading view of Speyside at Aviemore and the Grey Mountains beyond. Below our feet, the cliff falls sheer only for a short way and thereafter the perpendicular rocky wall gives place to a steep bank of scree on which the going is hard. Across the defile to the left, with a drop of 1,300 feet between, is the long, rounded form of Sron na Lairig, the Lairig's Nose, which projects from and partly conceals the mass of Braeriach. Behind us is the splendid cirque of Cairn Lochan, backed by Cairn Gorm's western corries, and thrusting its sharp brow beyond the Snowy Corrie is the Fiacill na Coire Cas (the Fiacill Ridge) which claims the Lurcher's name.

We turn our backs on the Lairig to walk down to the source of the stream which bears the Lurcher's name (Allt Creag na Leth-choin). We pass above the many springs from which Allt Creag na Leth-choin flows and move over among the white stones of the col, looking like seagulls in the distance, to the steep edge of the Lairig wall to see the Devil raise his Point five miles away beyond the watershed of the Pass. From this stance, the Devil's Point stands alone in the southern mouth of the Lairig, thrusting his prow forward from behind the intervening shoulder of Sron na Lairig and standing out sharp and black against the distant background of the Perthshire hills above Glen Tilt.

A high shoulder stands between us and the Cairn Lochan, which is the next picture we have a mind to see. After ten minutes climbing, we come out on the broad back and move due north along it to a little eminence marked by an egg-shaped ring on the Ordnance Survey map immediately to the left of the 'an' of Coire an Lochain. We go down some two hundred feet over rough boulder-ridden ground to find the best stance for a photograph of the lofty gallery of Cairn Lochan himself. Here we pause for breath once more. The pull up to the corner of Creag na Leth-choin and the ankle-twisting scramble along his anything-but-smooth backside have earned a draught from the flask and a smoke. Strict orthodoxy would forbid any such indulgence so early in the day but we are not seeking far horizons on this outing and relaxation is pleasant. Besides, it so happens that from this very boulder we look down on a burn which once provoked likely controversy over the origin of Cairngorm names. So we recall that battle of words long ago, reviving another memory of 1904.

I go back first to William Peyton once more, as leading witness in the case. When I was a little older than that day of the Robbers' Cave, he said to me, 'You know, Fred, climbing over the Cairngorms isn't the only thing you should do to them. I often take the map of a winter's night and live over again the kind of times we've had together. And I remember once, in Edinburgh, a long discussion going far into the night on the names on the map and how they got there.' No better subject for reminiscence and debate.

He said that he was first drawn to this business of Cairngorm names by the title of Cairn Gorm himself. Why should he have been christened 'The Cairn of the Azure Stone'? Neither he nor his partners in the range are blue, except at times in the transforming magic of the distant view, and the original Gaelic explicitly calls them red. They are the Monadh Ruadh —the Reds—in distinction from the Monadh Liaths—the Greys—on the western side of the Spey. The redness is derived from the presence of iron which gives its peculiar hue to the cairngorm stone itself, elsewhere called 'wine-coloured'. And the Gaelic pundit here breaks into the argument to remind us that 'gorm' means something more than 'blue', for it has a kind of secondary meaning of 'translucent', something which acquires more than the mere brightness of light by passing the rays through its own coloured prism. The mountain is thus beautifully named but in the translation from the musical Gaelic into English it becomes misnamed, and if we were at once more accurate and more poetic, we should anglicise him from the Gaelic into 'the Mountain of the Shining Stone'.

So much in reminiscence of Peyton.

This, and much more, was discussed on the boulder in 1904, and we were about to leap from it to continue on our upward way to Cairn Lochan, when:

'What's the name of that burn, anyway?' said one.

'Hasn't got one that I know, but it looks as if it came from Lochan Buidhe, round the corner of Cairn Lochan up there.'

'Does it? What d'you bet? It can't, in fact. 'Twould have to flow a mile uphill to do that.'

'Well, it's time it had a name and as you [meaning me] started us on the game, I move that we christen it Allt Geal or Allt Fionn: it looks white, anyway, the way it tumbles and bubbles about.'

The motion got no seconder and by the time we were on the banks of the little burn, we had spent a good part of the morning and were hungry. So we ate hard-boiled eggs, and started the broken shells on a race down a smooth quiet stretch of the burn where there was hardly any current at all. They were kittle cattle to enter for such a competition and most of them were quietly driven ashore by the breeze long before they reached the winning post. But, eventually, they all went to perdition in the broken water below.

'There!' I said. 'We've got the burn's name. It shall be called Allt Eggie.'

'Yes,' said the author of the first motion, 'and we'll have the deuce-an'-all fun with the cartographers when they try to decide how the deuce-an'-all the burn got its eggy name. No relation of Eigheach, the Brawling Burn of Rannoch, anyway.'

To this day, the map-makers have not been able to make up their minds between the claims of Allt Fionn and Allt Eggie.* And so, this little tributary of the Lurcher's Burn bears no name on any map except mine, as far as I know.

There is plenty of the explorer's zest to be found in pursuing to their origin the *authentic* names of stream and corrie in the Cairngorms. One needs the language for this and I am no Gaelic scholar or, as they would say, I 'have not the Gaelic'. All I ever knew, I first

*See Appendix Two

picked up from Donald Macrae of Glenelg, dressing 'cuddie-flies', repairing spars and pricking my fingers on fish-hooks on the Grunnd an Righ, the King's Ground, under the shadow of Wade's ruined barracks at Glenelg which look across Kyle Rhea to the Old Woman of Skye, though, to be sure, it is not certain that Wade himself built them. 'Tonald' was already near seventy and I was sixteen. He had seen the world in ships but was rarely provoked to speak of what he had seen. 'Och,' he would say, 'I wass at sea a while… but I'll no' be rememberin' very well, but a whiley back there was talk of a man called John Passificko… and they said there might be war and again there might not, and the recruitin' was going' on amang the fisherfolk, and I went… I wass no more than a laddie like yersel', but the life didna suit me in the fleet an' all… and after being at, what is't ye call it, Sa— Sa'stipol, down there… I just came home again. And there's no mistake about it, but Kerrara iss better than the foreign parts!'

Donald at seventy was still a powerful seaman-like figure, with strong gentle hands and full white beard, and from him I learned enough seafaring patter in his mother tongue for the needs of a lug-sail and the cutting of bait. A fine kedgeree of pidgin-Gaelic and schoolboy slang it was, and I can still hear his guffaws of delight at my way of saying things as we trolled for coalfish in the deep rapids of Kyle Rhea. And I learned some more from Angus, who told me in the Sound of Kerrera that the Harbour Master of Oban 'wass a great cod—*an trosg domhail*—that lived under dunollie... but nobody had effer catched him yet'; Angus whose inseparable companion was Bouskar, an Aberdeen terrier with white hairs in his tail, and one of these hairs 'in yer cuddie fly will mebbe get you a mackrel among the cuddies out there beyond the point'; Angus who could talk all four legs off a donkey and yarn you into a belief in anything.

But, for all Donald and Angus 'teached me in the Gaelic', it now fails me at times in judging Cairngorm names. And even though I went to school again in the Gaelic a dozen years later, with Fhir-an-Tigh as my tutor on Eilean Shona—Fhir-an-Tigh who could become Fhir-an-Tigh-an-Mara when needed for some of one hundred-and-one businesses of the sea, I have grown rusty since and I have to take MacAlpine and McKechnie from my shelf (these being the most inadequate 'Liddell and Scott' of the Gaelic) to find my way about in an almost-forgotten language.

In 1904 the Ordnance Survey prepared a Glossary

'primarily for the use of its own employees working in districts in which Gaelic place-names exist' and the Survey men were reminded that their unvarying rule must be to follow local custom, even where the academic purist in the Gaelic disapproved of popular spelling or pronunciation. In his preface to this Glossary, entitled 'The Explanation of the Most Common Gaelic Words, and Corrupted Forms of Gaelic, used on the Ordnance Survey Maps', compiled by John Mathieson, Civil Assistant, Ordnance Survey, Colonel Duncan A Johnston warned his men that 'no attempt should be made to alter corrupted forms into correct Gaelic unless the correct form is undoubtedly in general use; still less should names be altered (except on strong evidence) to conform to some supposed meaning.' Thus did the Survey wisely hold out against pedantry which would allow lexicographical exactitude to kill the living speech. And, believing the Colonel to be right, I have used the Ordnance Survey model.

As a matter of fact, no extensive Gaelic vocabulary is needed to find one's way among Cairngorm names. A page or two of print would hold them all. The Ordnance Survey Glossary of 1904 covers seven pages of printed foolscap and contains 328 entries.

This is, of course, an arbitrary minimum and it does not cover all the names that the map reviser would have to know, but is perhaps to be regarded as Basic Gaelic for Cairngorm topography. The Scottish Mountaineering Club have a more exacting standard, albeit their Gaelic editor accepts the Ordnance Survey spelling as a working basis, and so may we. But, whatever guide he followed, unless one has the 'feel' of the words, all the flitting shadows of meaning that throng around them are lost and the use of any one of them to describe a mountain, a stream, or a person thus fails to carry to the mind the associations that belong to it. All words, and notably the common coin of ordinary speech, bear their associations in echoes and shadows of fuller meaning within and around them. So it is with the Gaelic, which has woven a unique poetic and historic garment round its most expressive words and reveals its texture, as it were, in the haunting music of Gaelic sound.

This kind of appreciation is needed to grasp the full sense, as well as the harmonies in a minor key, of Highland speech. But it helps us very little in the search for the origins of the names. As Peyton said, 'The fun is to find out how they got there.' Mons Graupius, Etchachan, Dhondail and the Coire au

Tailleur—not only what they mean but why the names stuck where they did. Highland legend gives some clues, as in the case of the Coire au Saighdeir, the Soldier's Corrie, which falls like a curtain of rock between Carn Toul and the Devil's Point, and it is easy to see why no less than three streams bear the lovely name of Luineag. But why is Corrie Gorm not on Cairn Gorm himself? And how did Beinn Muich Dhui permit one of the smaller fry to usurp the name of Monadh Mor which belongs to him by right? Or again, why does Sgoran Dubh allow *his* lesser neighbour to steal the title 'The Great', at least in the Bartholomew maps, when in fact Sgoran Dubh Mor is a whole twenty-three feet lower than himself? Here is the fun that William Peyton sought when he sat with friends over his log fire in a Broughty Ferry winter.

So much for Allt Eggie and his name—and this almost unpardonably long digression. If we had been on far horizons bent, we should never have let the hours pass in such diversions and excursions to the sources of nowhere. It was just as well that we had no fixed goal in our minds that day: true acquaintance with the Cairngorms requires the wanderer, now and then, to let the day look after itself and, while it lasts, wander at will, breaking off at a tangent to follow a bird or stream in and out of hidden corners.

It was already early afternoon when we reached, as we thought, the true source of Allt Eggie in the tiny lochan in Coire an Lochain itself, which is below Cairn Lochan, but whether the crest at the head of the corrie takes its name from the loch or vice versa is hard to say. No dispute arose among us whether this hen or that egg came first, for we had no sooner decided that the lochan was Allt Eggie's source than we saw the 'wee wee burn' running into the upper end and realised that it must rise still higher up. On our way, it disappeared but, almost on the same level, we found *another* burn flowing the wrong way down from the right into another lochan, the kidney-shaped tarn right under the western cliffs of Coire Carn an Lochan, this being the true Tarn-of-the-Corrie-of-the-Cairn-of-the-Tarn. This second burn emptied itself into the lochan at what by all reasonable reckoning should have been its lower end, and it never came out again on the surface. It must drain out of the bottom of the tarn, and if you listen you can hear it talking underground before it reappears in order to flow into the tinier lochlet below.

One needs even more than the one-inch map to see clearly this little corner of Cairngorm geography and why three active young men spent the best part of two hours upon the exploration of a nameless burn.

We complete the pilgrimage to Allt Eggie's true birthplace by climbing some five hundred feet up the sheer western end of the corrie. Besides us, the little stream is now a white streak of cataract tumbling down the steep flank of Cairn Lochan, and there is more water in this fall than runs out of the lochan below. For every gallon that is now foaming past us, not more than a quart comes out of the first lochan to run down to the second, our Hen Tarn, and we saw, or rather heard, the other three quarts running their subterranean course out of sight between the two lochans. The actual spot where she first comes to light lies at 3,500 feet in a little bevy of springs bearing a family resemblance to those of the Lurcher's Burn. Her true source lies in a secluded amphitheatre where a steep bank of lush grass grows exactly on the 3,500-foot contour, the water trickling out in a score of tiny channels that wander at will down the gentlest slope till they join to make a stream of crystal water flowing in broad shallows, with pleasant deep little narrow pools between them, and in places moving so slowly that the hot June sun warms the water many degrees above the cold spring only a few yards higher up. At her source Allt Eggie is a true *fuaran*, a cold well bubbling to the surface in water more refreshing than any found in the plains, but after being warmed almost to brackishness, it does not regain its first coolness till it has come out of the two lochans five hundred feet below.

This was truly an Allt Gun Ainm—a nameless burn—till we found a name for it, and the memory of that idle but lively moment under the shadow of Cairn Lochan has stayed with me through forty years. Trifles have a knack of clinging to the mind and of giving a clue to the identity of a person or the setting of some otherwise forgotten event, and matters of great moment have sometimes turned on trifles. In this Cairngorm chronicle, Allt Eggie begins with a trifle, an eggshell, but each time I have returned to the scene and climbed to the cluster of springs where the burn first comes out of its green source, I have seen more than I saw at first. There is a quality in the setting of Allt Eggie's spring which Browning described as 'silent and aware'. The little stream runs its course to the edge of Cairn Lochan's steep side without the rippling murmur and gurgle that gives the name *caochan* to other highland burns. It flows in silence and in solitude, and even after the heaviest rain its clear water grows neither turgid nor turbulent. I have seen it in wet weather and in dry, and always it holds its smooth course undisturbed. The crystal mirror remains undimmed.

But the stream alone is not the secret of the spell which this secluded corner may cast upon the wayfarer. Without Allt Eggie, the scene would not be what it is, no doubt, for Allt Eggie is at once the finishing touch and the signpost pointing to the whole picture and to the frame in which Nature's cunning has set it. It is the wholeness of the picture that arrests the eye and stays in the mind. What you see before you is an amphitheatre, grey with granite and green with the mossy grass, flanking with its enclosing sides the source of the stream, a low terrace set against the steep stony slope that falls rapidly from the *miadan* of the Lurcher's Crag. Out of the same womb Allt Eggie emerges unique, but it is the composition of the picture, the perfect proportion and harmony of all its parts, that makes the appeal to the eye and stamps the impression on the mind. It is this harmony which the Chinese express in their two characters Feng Shui, which literally mean wind–water but which, when applied to the site of a temple or a family grave, denote a place made fit for its sacred office by the harmonious co-operation of the forces of nature. Whether such Chinese scenes when I first saw them reminded me of Allt Eggie's birthplace or whether, on returning from the East, I found a reminder of them in this Cairngorm stream, I do not know.

And so we move round the 3,500-foot contour, and climb another 483 feet to the high rim of Cairn Lochan in order to look down on the scene of Allt Eggie's first journey down the hill. We spend a few moments verifying his short course and conducting a brief ceremony of initiation and baptism, with inaccurate quotations of 'O Fons Bandusiae'. Allt Eggie may not be 'more resplendent than crystal', but our association with him deserves an ode and Horace will do as well as another.

Here on Cairn Lochan, we are on a platform of granite which is both a spectacle in itself and an outlook tower giving a wide view around it. There are few finer crests in the whole range of the Cairngorms, and the spreading scene across four counties with the sparkling waters of the Moray Firth beyond rivals the northern panorama of Cairn Gorm itself. Geologically, Cairn Lochan and his two great corries may be no more than one of the battlements of Cairn

Gorm, but they have good claims of their own; in fact, the Cairn's crest and his almost unique rockface below are conspicuous features in the picture of the whole range seen from Aviemore. We could see from below, when we were mainly concerned with Allt Eggie (and have proved it since), that the sloping corrie wall is as interesting to the student as to the climber of rocks. Not only does the corrie put his namesake of Braeriach in the shade, but there are striking examples of the Great Mason's chisel in the square-hewn rocks at the top and a steep slab of bare red rock about half-way down, just when the cliff breaks into scree, which has been called 'a unique curtain'. A great gut called The Vent leads up the left side of the slab. These features give Cairn Lochan a place of his own in the grand panorama of the High Cairngorms, but you must find them for yourself and appraise them from above and below, else you may easily dismiss them merely as the flanking wall of Cairn Gorm's western defences. Cairn Lochan is all that, but he is much more than that and will reveal how much more on close acquaintance, as certain latter-day climbers have proved when they visited him with intent to discover the secrets of his Vents, his Gullies and his Buttresses.

Having a pleasant and deliberate freedom from the exacting duty of 'getting to the top', we turn away from Cairn Lochan to fix the exact spot of the watershed in the high tableland stretching south from Cairn Lochan to Ben Macdhui. Watersheds make as good a pastime for vagrant folk on the hills as any other occupation; none better indeed, for you can never be *quite* sure where to place them. This leaves room for dispute and the dissection of evidence, for little bets and large claims of conscience. But today's little exercise in topographical research will, I guess, be soon over, for there should be little doubt where this Avon–Dee watershed lies.

Following the county border between Banff and Inverness to the point where the Aberdeen border joins it and the three counties meet at 3,900 feet, we come in sight of Lochan Buidhe, from which the Avon (in the form of Feith Buidhe) starts on its way to the Moray Firth. The tarn is two hundred feet below us and some seven hundred yards away. Sitting on one of those tufts of black moss, with our feet on the gritty granite gravel, we turn the glasses on the little sheet of brown water, and I will swear that this Buidhe feeds not one stream but two. For, while Feith Buidhe flows almost due east out of the tawny tarn, the March Burn flows due west from the same point and, as everyone knows, the March Burn is one of the sources of the Dee.

'Fiddlesticks,' says Hugh, 'it's as plain as anything that the March Burn isn't coming out of the Buidhe Lochan. The Feith Burn does, but I can see quite distinctly that the March has a spring of its own.'

Inspection on the spot must surely silence contention. But, in the event, it does nothing of the kind. The first evidence seemed to support Hugh's claim, for the March Burn came to the surface in a source some little distance away. But there was nothing to choose in difference of level between the two and I maintained that, after heavy rain, the lochan might expand and rise enough to cover both.

'Mebbe,' retorted Hugh, 'but not as we see it. And that's what the bet was about.'

'Yes,' said McGilky. 'That bet's lost.'

So it was paid, but if I had stated my claim in a slightly different way, I could not have lost, the truth being that all the surface water of this watershed between Ben Macdhui and Cairn Gorm probably rises from one underground reservoir. It is only the chance formation of the rock beneath that sends Feith to the surface in a spring under the tarn and March to the surface in a spring of his own. And, as if to clinch the matter, the Scottish Mountaineering Club speaks of our lochan as 'a tiny pool which drains into the Feith Buidhe and Loch Avon but might almost equally well flow into the March Burn'.

Allt Eggie and the watershed controversy between them have swallowed up a good part of the day and signs of changing weather behind Ben Macdhui look like rain coming up from Braemar. We take the hint and follow the March Burn down its steep course, set in scree and loose stones, to the bed of the Lairig where it disappears for a while, only to reappear in the well-known Pools of Dee. We are not following the Dee today but, returning north-west across the pass at 2,700 feet, we make our way back to Rothiemurchus. Had we yielded to our first temptation and set out for the summit of Ben Macdhui after the watershed bet was lost and won, we should not have come home dry. For, when we turned at the head of the pass to look back at the heavy flank of the mountain behind us, the mist was rolling in thick folds over the rocks above the Tailors' Burn and the air in the Lairig turned cold with a strong breeze blowing up from the south-east.

Rough weather in the mountains has its own

rewards, though no one climbing in the Cairngorms will go out of his way to meet the storm. One asks for fine weather from them but a spell of fine weather is almost certain to break in storm. The longer the spell, and the hotter the season, the more certain it is that, when it comes, the storm will show you something to remember.

One such occasion came in the same summer of 1904, above the western shoulder of Cairn Gorm himself which goes by the name of Sron an Aonach, the Nose-that-Stands-by-Itself. We had come down from the cairn at the end of one of June's hottest days. By late afternoon, the air grew heavy and though there was no sign to the north or to the west that the weather would break, the sky behind us to the east was already looking sickly. The light breeze had failed altogether and the sparkling brightness of the day was faintly dimmed. Before long, out of nowhere it seemed, the coming event began to cast its pale shadow before it with that sense of something uncanny impending, when the air is laden with suspense and a stillness which portends a storm.

The nearer objects stood out more clearly than ever and the rocks of Coire na Ciste seemed to grow longer and sharper in the changing light. The very heaven seemed to be closing in upon us, lower and lower overhead, surrounding us with oppression, like the cells of an invisible prison. The usual fresh colours faded from the heavy sky into the olive-green-ochre of a bruise on flesh.

That was how Charlotte Brontë saw them in the gathering storm on the heath in *Shirley*:

'I know how the Heath would look on such a day,' said Caroline Helstone. 'Purple-black, a deeper shade of sky-tint, and that would be livid.'

To which Shirley:

'Yes: quite livid, with brassy edges to the clouds, and here and there a white gleam more ghastly than the livid tinge which, as you looked at it, you momentarily expected would kindle into blinding lightning.'

One may see and feel something of this on the eve of any thunderstorm anywhere, but only when one is under the powerhouse of the electric storm in the High Cairngorms does one have the sensation that something has upset the balance of things, that the law of gravity itself is losing its grip and the world might turn upside down if the disturbance were to prevail much longer. To point the contrast of peace and war, we could see under the edge of the breaking storm, beyond the rift of the Slugan Pass, a glimpse of Strathspey landscape towards Boat of Garten still unclouded and full of sunlight so sparkling that this little window into brightness only served to darken the deep shades around us.

A Cairngorm storm comes up in this fashion, almost in silence. And just when the tension seems almost unbearable, the storm breaks. 'There is a sudden wind among these stones that can cast men down on the stillest day.' So said the Betah after watching Kim and the Lama come down over the Black Breasts of Eua, and the climber, pausing in a moment of suspense on the threshold of the tempest, knows that his words were true. This is sober fact, not novelist's fancy. Every mountaineer knows that the power of the wind on the heights is irresistible and he knows, too, that the descriptions and estimates of velocity in the Beaufort scale are only true at sea level.

In this respect, 1947 must have been an exceptional year, for on April 21st, June 27th and July 17th, wind-speeds over 80 mph were reported in several parts of the British Isles, and at Mildenhall the gauge at 9.20 pm on June 27th reached 98 mph. On our heights, these velocities are not rarities and Dr Buchan has reported gusts over 150 mph at the top of Ben Nevis. Moreover, it is not only on the summit that the wind blows with hurricane force. Wherever it is penned in by high walls of rock, say, at the watershed of the Lairig Pass just north of the Pools of Dee, it blows with concentrated fury which has probably never been measured, though often felt.

The storm itself breaks in a blast of icy wind, tearing the grey-ochre sky with a crackling blinding flash of lightning. In a moment, the concealed batteries of the clouds open fire, crack-crack-crashing round the hilltop and rumbling in half-smothered detonations in the hidden corrie. The plainsman often speaks of the deafening, blinding storm but nowhere in flat country will your ears be split and your skin become gooseflesh as in one of these electric storms in the higher Grampians. ''Tis only in the high hills that the thunderbolts fall.' And there are certain danger spots (Carn a' Mhaim is said to be one of them, and Sgor Gaoith another) where you had best not be caught when the storm breaks, but if you are near enough, yet not too near, you will have a feast of sight and sound to be remembered for many a day.

In the midst of it one may perceive what the poet of Psalm CL meant by 'the firmament of His Power'. Sky and air seem to surround you with a swaying enwreathing curtain, billowing around and beneath, as if the blast of Advent blew o'er Horeb, and the shrieking wind rushes at you from all sides at once.

The heavy sky that could not weep
Is loosened: rain falls steep
And thirty singing furies ride
To split the sky from side to side.

Once, from the rim of Braeriach's Coire Brochain, I watched a thunderstorm come up from the south-east, delivering its first attack—a mere feint— on Monadh Mor, and then gathering its force for the main assault, falling in concentrated fury on Sgor an Lochain Uaine. Carn Toul, which a few moments before had been a dark roof under a canopy of menacing cloud, was obliterated. The rain fell in a black curtain, concealing the Angel, the Devil and the Twin Gables between, and for a full half-hour these peaks were battered by artillery and drenched with the flood. Though we were a mile away and the thunder never came overhead, rain enough there was, to be sure, and we were drenched too. Before the storm abated, little streaks of white water were pouring in Corrie Brochain under our feet, while the Dee in Garbh Corrie Dhe was roaring down the corrie wall to the right in a cataract swollen to many times its puny size of an hour before.

The storm had a remarkable aftermath. It was late afternoon. The day had been heavy and warm, with bright sunshine on the northern corries of Braeriach and the gathering tempest to the east and the south. When the rain stopped, the sun shone bright and strong behind us but there were still the remains of the storm to be swept up by the wind from the Rough Corrie of the Dee and Coire Brochain. It was still black over Carn Toul, whose double head loomed eerily out of a dark rift in the waning storm till it looked like 'the black horns of Raieng where you hear the whistle of the wild goats through the clouds'. And when the last reverberation of thunder had died away somewhere under Carn Toul's steep side, heavy banks of cloud still lingered between us and Glen Dee. One by one, they were caught by the wind and driven in streamers and pennants and rolling waves up the Porridge Cauldron (Coire Brochain), and as they poured up the narrowing gulf like 'the playthings of nature's mischief', we saw long dark streaks and patches on them as they rose out of the shadow beneath into the sunlight in which we stood. We were at first puzzled by the fact that the dark streaks did not move upwards with the racing mist. They floated on the surface, changing shape, disappearing, then reappearing in the same place but always returning to their original shape, no matter how wraith-like they might seem in that insubstantial pageant of cloud. Suddenly we realised that they were our shadows cast on the rushing mist by the sun behind us but, by some trick or cloud-shape, they were magnified many times, so that it was little wonder that we failed to recognise our small selves in those giant figures thrown on the screen of the mist. They were indeed mist shadows that 'look not like / The inhabitants o' the earth'.

Our Long Grey Men of Corrie Brochain were gone with the wind. Soon not a wrack was left behind in the Porridge Cauldron beneath us, and only in the broadened streak of silver that marked the flow of the Dee from the Wells away to the right was there evidence that the heavens were opened only a short while ago. How much water falls during one of these violent short-lived storms I do not know, and only on Ben Nevis is there a rain gauge to measure it. But no gauge is needed to reveal its effects or the force of its attack on some of its targets. Many a climber has seen the plateau of Ben Macdhui covered with hailstones a couple of inches deep, varying in size from a pea to a sparrow egg, after a twenty-minute downpour, though, to be sure, it is no *down*pour but is usually driven aslant the hill with such violence by the squall that one must find shelter or be sorely bruised before it is over. One witness said that he had been caught in a storm on Ben Macdhui, 'with great lumps of ice in it and lightning you could feel warm on your face'.

Even if the storm only brings rain, the icy battery will sting the skin till it smarts again, and the usually glib words 'soaked to the skin' mean exactly what they say. The rain falls, not in sheets, but in unbroken lines of opaque whiteness which soon form an impenetrable curtain round the cairn. But when the storm has passed, most of the water has vanished underground to fill the cisterns that feed the permanent springs from which the Druie, the Dee and the Avon flow. Enough remains above-ground to fill the depressions with wide shallow pools, and Lochan Buidhe, the highest little sheet of water in all the Cairngorms, is one of these. Springs break out and rivulets flow where no water ran an hour before. If you stand on Carn Toul, you will see the whole eastern rockface of the Lairig Pass streaked with a score of new cataracts, while March Burn and the Tailor are swollen to cascades of white. And the air is filled with the music of waterfalls.

In volume and intensity, though not in duration and extent, these sudden storms rival the torrential rains that accompany the typhoon in the China Seas. James Brown's long-forgotten Deeside Guide—he was not its real author, by the way—tells how one of them invaded Ballater in 1829:

For some time previous there had been more than a common downfall of rain, and in especial the day before, the rain had been pouring down in one incessant torrent; there had been heard the rumblings of many fierce thunderclaps ... Nowise alarmed, the people of Ballater went to their beds as usual but at midnight they were awakened by the terrible roaring of the river ... the rush of the waters was heard near at hand, and, in a handclap, in it swept with a furious swirl breaking in waves over the very beds where the people lay aquaking ... Then suddenly they started up, and rushed out from their houses naked and unclothed, shouting and lamenting when they beheld on all sides of them nothing but a great sea of troubled waters, upon which they saw floating sheet, hayricks, great trees torn up by the roots, chairs, tables, eight-day clocks, and all sorts and manner of things, while always the river was roaring on like thunder … the river continued to rise higher and higher still; greater lots of trees, bushes, and other wood began to gather about the arches of the bridge … and at last the waters were so dammed up that no power on earth could withstand them, and the first sign that the bridge was falling was a loud crack which it was heard to give, as loud as the report of a musket. Then the solid masonry of the bridge was seen slowly to bend like a bow of fir, till, with a noise like that of the loudest thunder, it flew from each other into a thousand bits, and was hurled with a plash into the river to be seen no more.

A century later, the memorial of this night's work could still be seen in the waste of shingle and stones that fills the angle where the Quoich falls into the Dee.

These sudden storms break with great violence. They can undermine and shear away the looser upper scree of the hillside, leaving a deep wound. The 'watcher' of former days in the Corrour Bothy vouches for simultaneous landslides on the Devil's Point and Carn a' Mhaim on opposite sides of the upper Dee, let loose by unprecedented cloudburst. His words sound as if he had been the eyewitness of a scene which re-enacted in miniature the famous landslide in that best of all Kipling stories, 'The Miracle of Purun Bhagat'. And the place from which he 'saw the mountain falling' recalls the testimony of many witnesses that Carn a' Mhaim is one of the most notable centres of electric disturbance in the whole Grampian range. We have already found that Carn a' Mhaim has a magnetism of her own. And it may be—why not?—that there is some link between her power to draw the lightning from the sky and her power over us.

Epilogue
The Curtain Falls in Glen Einich

The scene of the epilogue of this chronicle is the narrow waist of Glen Einich, where the broken waters of the Bennie Burn (Am Beanidh) pour through the gap between Cadha Mor and Carn Elrig. We had bicycled from the Dell of Rothiemurchus (or the Manse of Insh) to a point just below the last clump of trees on the banks of the stream and, leaving the path, we set out to cross the burn opposite Carn Elrig itself. From the left bank, I jumped to a flat boulder in midstream and in doing so stirred up an injury to my right knee which I had twisted six years before over a sandbag in the London Blitz and Black-Out of 1940. The original injury had cost me ten days in hospital but now it was to cost me a deal more. Once on the flat boulder, I knew my knee would carry me up no more hills that day. It could not even brace itself to the second and longer jump to the right bank of the Bennie Burn. So I stayed where I was, on the flat boulder, with the brown water gurgling round me and the cloudless September sky overhead.

Behind me the line of Cadha Mor stretched past Coutt's Stone (why do some call it the Atholl Stone?) to Sgoran Dubh. The characteristic buttresses of the Sgoran Dubh–Sgor Gaoith wall over Loch Einich rose above the nearer skyline of the west slope of Carn Elrig and the moraine which lies across the glen. They were thus screened from view for the most part. But the glass showed clearly the upper part of the first and finest buttress, with its steep chimney leading to the crest and the massive masonry which rivals even the giant piles of Lochnagar and Cairn Lochan. As I turned to get a steadier view through the binoculars, a sharp twinge in my knee reminded me why I was not already half-way up Carn Elrig, why I was lamely looking at these familiar hills, not climbing them. And, as if to give sharper point to the reminder, the golden eagle that has his eyrie under Sgor Gaoith soared into the sky above the loch, showing the flange of his tawny wing in the sunlight as he swept in a beautiful turning movement round the cirque of Corrie Odhar and disappeared in the direction of Braeriach's Old Man (Am Bodach) who looks west across Loch Einich to his partner A'Cailleach, the Old Woman of Sgor Gaoith.

It was teasing enough to see the familiar summit

of Sgoran Dubh standing back from the steep buttressed wall that rises from Glen Einich, tantalising enough in all conscience to sit on a rock in the bed of the Bennie Burn and realise that the planned circuit of the day's outing could not be followed, but most frustrating of all the sights in that brief sojourn on the midstream stone was that the eagle could see what I had never seen, and could never see—the spreading panorama of Einich in a bird's eye view. True, I have since been fortunate enough to secure a bird's eye view of the whole Cairngorm scene in the form of an air photograph taken by the Royal Air Force in pursuit of their own lawful occasions. But, as I sat constricted and restrained on my flat boulder, I could only feel that the golden eagle was sent as a painful reminder of the littleness of man. There in the blue September sky was the very picture and emblem of effortless flight: the golden eagle sweeping round the great circuit of the Einich hills and never for one moment pausing to reflect that the poor biped marooned on that rock in the bed of the Bennie Burn must, even in full exercise of sinew and brawn, spend many hours in traversing the same scene.

When we set out in the early morning, we had no precise object in view—nothing more and nothing less than another long day on the hills. But, as we came up through the autumn-coloured forest, I was drawn to the old circuit from the bed of the Bennie Burn under Cadha Mor, up Carn Elrig, across Carn a' Phris-ghuibhais and the Little Bennie Burn to the grand Corrie Lochain of Braeriach and so on, past the Bogha-cloich corrie and the edge of Corrie Dhondail to the crest of Corrie Odhar above Loch Einich, and home again by Sgor Gaoith, Sgoran Dubh, the Coutts and Argyll Stones to Cadha Mor and the narrowing gut of Glen Einich once more. But man proposes… and the London Black-Out disposes. So I was left, a marooned and helpless spectator of a scene in which I had designed to be an actor, and remained a disabled onlooker.

That sailing golden eagle seemed to have been sent to rub it in. He could survey the scene with little effort. He could turn whither fancy or appetite led. I could not. I was tethered to my boulder. But I had one advantage and superiority over him, that even if disabled I could summon many moving mountain memories to palliate the frustration of a useless limb. Were he so disabled, that would be his end, even if he went down fighting. No doubt, as he circles and soars over the great gulf and cirque of Einich, he can see what I can never see but he cannot find solace, in all his wide sweep over the Cairngorms, in the words that rise to my lips as I look up to Braeriach and Sgor Gaoith:

But, as for me, at least with maimed delight,
Still let me love, though I may not possess.

London
December 1943–1947

Appendix I
The Herring Bap & Old Moorland

And here a different cause of debate: what to eat on the hill? Hard-boiled eggs, of course, sandwiches of ham or egg or liver sausage or jam, bittersweet chocolate and those round hard peppermints which give the needed sugar, and so on, with a word in favour of (mine is against) tomatoes, messy things on the hill anyway! But I am alone in my taste for the Herring Bap, an unusual sandwich which deserves a word of advertisement. If I were a nineteenth-century writer of dialectic habit, I would commence my advocacy of the Herring Bap by saying, 'Dear Reader, I begin my plea for this succulent and edible victual…' and I am inclined to carry on in this vein but refrain. I leave the formality of prose in order to say, 'If you don't know the bap, you ought to.' It is a wheaten-flour roll made by Scottish bakers, who always beat their English namesakes, no one knows why, and for all I know it may have an inferior English equivalent with an English name. But, lest you should have lived so long without getting your teeth into a bap,

I take the liberty of telling you that it is an oval sort of roll, fat enough to make your mouth open wide to seize it and with a brownish (not too brown) skin just resistant enough (no one dare call it tough) to make you bite, as only hungry hill-teeth can bite. So much for the container. Now we pass to consider what it contains. In preparing the Herring Bap, you tear out most of the soft inside of the bap, and put it aside. Then you put soused herring into the space thus left vacant—and it will take three herrings to fill it. If your herring are properly soused, they will taste better than sea-trout, much better, and you can take it from me that a proper HB will house at least three of them, and will make a better hill meal than anything else.

But we have left unused what Hamlet would call 'the guts' of the bap. If you are a frugal person, you will wish to find a use for these *ejecta viscera* of the now complete Herring Bap. And you will use them, or it, by taking the rolling pin and flattening out the succulent guts of the bap till they are spread on the board in a thinnish layer of scone, as it were. The next stage is to break up bits of plain chocolate (for this I prefer Terry's bittersweet drops, if I have the right tradename) and spread them over the guts of the bap, roll the whole thing into a kind of chocolate sausage… and you have the best possible second course of your meal on the hills. I have done twelve hours in the High Cairngorms on two baps treated thus and, once more, *experto crede*.

I confess that I have not persuaded most, or any, of my partners on the hill to follow my example of the Herring Bap, but I call it a winner nonetheless. I will never take the road to the High Cairngorms with anything else in my pocket and, claiming no copyright in this design of nutrition, I leave it to you. With a final word on drink.

Nowhere in the world will you find better water than in any of the hundreds of Allts and trickles and springs of the Grampians. And, on most days in the hills, you will need nothing more. But there is always the Uisgebagh to be carried as reinforcement on occasion. You will have your own taste in this Scottish gift to the world. I have mine and I always carry a flask of Old Moorland, blended by a friend and former political opponent in the City of Perth.

There is a story worth telling about the man who first made Old Moorland. A fire in the bonded warehouse destroyed the bulk of his season's stock as it was about to go on the market. The stock was not large, but represented a year's trade in whisky of high quality. Next morning one of the greater distillers, condoling with him, said, 'Can I help you out? You can have anything you want from our stock, just to tide you over.' The old man looked across his mahogany desk in silence for a moment. Then he said, 'Verra kind o' ye, verra thochtful Ah'm sure, Mr —. But ye ken fine, your stuff's no' guid enough for me.' And the son of the big distiller, in telling the story, added, 'And, damn it all, the old man was right.'

Appendix II
Putting Allt Eggie on the Map

That is not the end of the story! Later research will show that Allt Eggie became the consecrated name. For, on his induction to the Post of Hill Warden, an honorific title conferred on the retiring incumbent when he vacates the Chair of Geology and Stone-Lore in the University of St Regulus, the Professor-Emeritus had this to say:

'It is not easy, Mr Vice-Chancellor, to find new ways of approach to my subject. And I may perhaps be absolved from the search on the ground that my long tenure of the Chair, which I now with equal regret and relief vacate, has given me full opportunity to exhaust myself and the patience of my classes upon it. By the fiat of our Royal Founder, I leave the Chair only to become Hill Warden, an office which, in no mere figure of speech, is as great as your own, for it makes me Vice-Chancellor of the Rig-Monadh. I thus take a new lease of life and my tongue must wag once more upon an old theme. I have spent much labour upon the

scientific foundation of geology, and now I leave the fruits of that labour, such as they are, to be gathered by my successor whom I rejoice to welcome today. And I turn from the stricter service of science to the looser play of mere words. By which I mean that, as Hill Warden, I offer myself the entertainment of studying at leisure and without academic compulsion, the nomenclature of the Cairngorms, on which a prophetic threat within me foreshadows the publication of a book bearing that title, if indeed I shall live to finish it.'

The veteran Professor then delivered his well-known Apostrophe to the Hills, which, by universal testimony, deeply moved his hearers. In the course of his Bird's Eye View of the Cairngorms—'and his winged words were like the flight of an eagle'—he came to the very spot where the burn behind Creag na Leth-choin once took its nameless way. The thread of his discourse continues:

'We have all observed that certain names repeat themselves, sometimes more than once, all over the Cairngorms. I do not know—I ought to but I don't—how many Ben Mores there are in all Scotland, but I do know that there are at least three Luineags, two Lairigs, several Geal Charns, not

to speak of the many Coire an Lochains, in the Cairngorms, alone. Moreover, in the case we now reach, there is an instance of how accident and the corroding drift of circumstance may mix names and confuse identities. Frequenters of the western spur of Cairn Gorm itself know well the beetling brow which is called Creag na Leaceann, anglice, *the Lurcher's Crag. And some may know that this bastion above the Lairig Ghru gives its name to a stream that rises from its backward parts; but few are they who know that another stream joins the Allt Creag na Leaceann soon after its birth. This latter watercourse is the occasion of that confusion of identity to which I drew your attention a moment ago. For many years it ran its nameless course unheeded, rising almost at the very feet of Cairn Lochan and running steeply down till it joined the other stream. So it had run through the ages; so, haply might it have run forever, unconscious of any deprivation because, though marked on every map, it never had a name. But, Mr Vice-Chancellor, private research has revealed to me not only that it has borne a name for well nigh sixty years, but also the manner in which the name was acquired. As you shall hear!*

I possess an old copy of the earlier one-inch Ordnance Survey Map of the Cairngorms, dated somewhere in the early nineteen-hundreds. And upon it the little thread of this stream is marked ALLT EGGIE, not by the printer, but in faded ink in the writing of the previous owner of the map. This led me to speculate on the origin of the name and I naturally had recourse to competent Gaelic authorities, to know whether it might have some connection with other names of a similar root and sound. There is of course Beinn Eighe in the north west, and there is each, *the Gaelic word for horse, which might have become corrupted in its journey to Cairn Lochan. But horses and Coire an Lochain do not go well together, and so our combined ingenuity could forge no satisfactory link between the known and the unknown. And I had almost forgotten the matter when, following my usual custom of a Saturday afternoon, I was browsing in Messrs Leabhar and Reiceadair's well-stocked shop and I lighted upon a tattered copy of a small volume, now long out of print, on the Cairngorms by an entirely unknown writer of the name of Whyte. And there I found the story of Allt Eggie. The book was published in 1944 and here we are, nearly a generation later, unearthing evidence of the way in which one feature in the Cairngorms acquired its name. I shall pursue the elucidation of the point at my leisure, but for the present I may be allowed to wonder with you how many other features in these great mountains owe their titles to such trifles.* Parturient montes, nasceture ridiculus mus!'

For the next few moments the old Professor related the incident of our eggshell race in 1904 and, with his aid, our light-hearted christening ceremony put Allt Eggie literally 'on the map', for he secured the adoption of the name which was printed thereafter on every Cairngorm map.

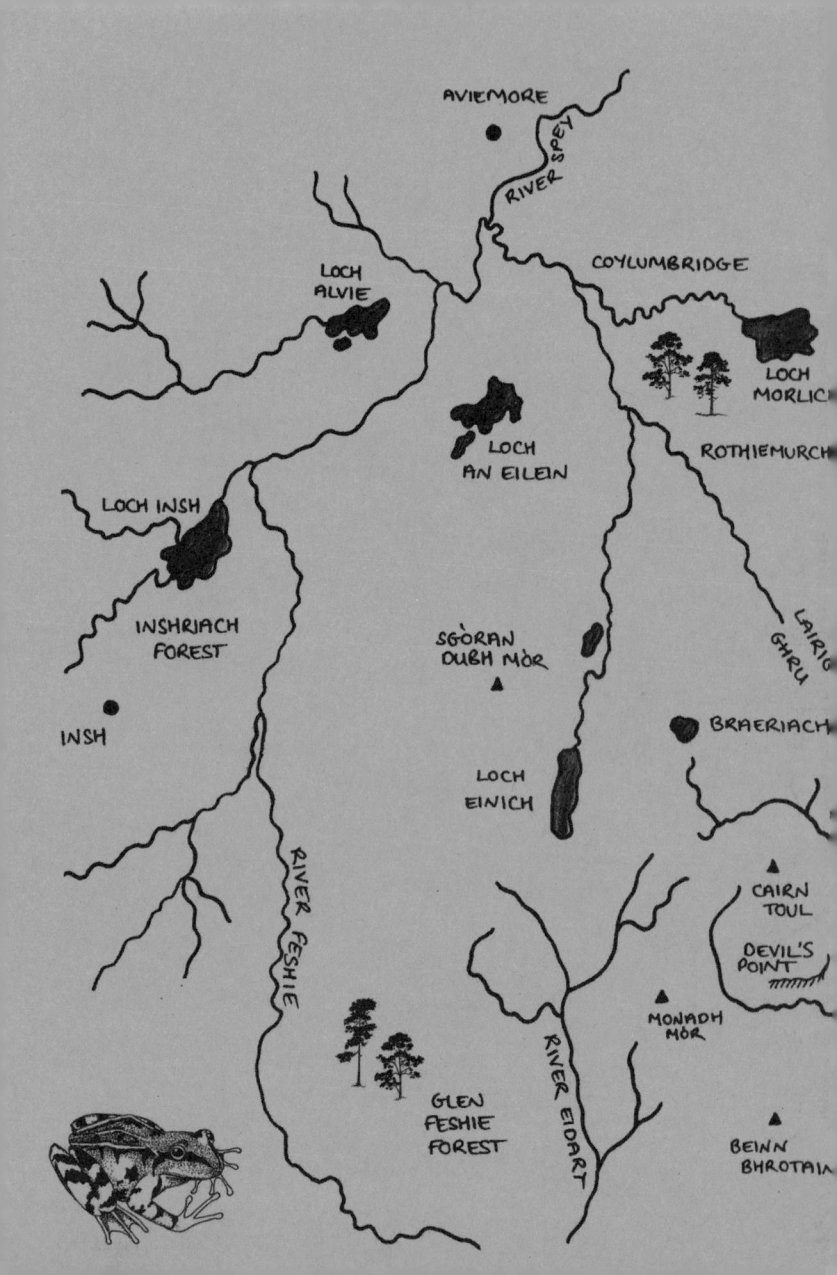